BASIC VOCABULARY IN EVERYDAY ENGLISH

BASIC VOCABULARY IN EVERYDAY ENGLISH

QUESTION OF THE DAY
READ/LISTEN AND UNDERSTAND
MAIN STORY
VOCABULARY USE IN DIALOG
FINAL REVIEW

박수정 지음

HANYANG UNIVERSITY PRESS

본 교재는 일상생활에서 자주 사용되는 어휘와 자주 접하게 되는 주제를 중심으로 기본적인 의사소통이 가능하도록 하는 데 학습 목표를 두고 있습니다. 교재 전반부에서는 영어의 기본 동사를, 교재 후반부에서는 일상적인 주제와 관련된 어휘 및 표현들을 다루었으며 각 단원별 구체적인 학습 내용과 순서는 다음과 같습니다.

QUESTION OF THE DAY		목표 어휘에 대한 자가진단 목적의 질의응답식 발화 활동
READ/LISTEN AND UNDERSTAND		목표 어휘가 읽기/대화 지문에서 어떻게 사용되는지 쓰임새 확인
MAIN STORY		
	WORD/THEME STUDY	목표 어휘의 세부적인 의미와 용법 학습
	IDIOMS AND PROVERBS	예시 문장을 통한 숙어와 속담의 의미 유추
	PHRASAL VERBS	대화문을 이용한 구동사의 의미 유추 및 용법 학습
	THIS IS CONFUSING!	목표 어휘와 관련된 학습자들의 궁금증 해결
	VARIETY/REGISTER/NUANCE	목표 어휘의 지역별/상황별 사용 및 뉘앙스 이해
	WORD PARTS	접사/문맥을 이용한 새로운 어휘의 의미 유추
VOCABULARY USE IN DIALOG		특정 맥락의 대화에서의 어휘 사용 연습
FINAL REVIEW		간단한 문장 형태의 영작을 통한 학습 내용 복습

이와 같이 본 교재의 특징은 초급 수준의 학습자들이 새로운 어휘의 의미 및 용법을 유추할 때 문맥을 통해 좀 더 효율적으로 학습하도록 한 데 있으며, 이렇게 학습한 어휘의 적용 역시 실용적인 상황 속에서 발화될 수 있도록 학습 과정을 구성했습니다. 아무쪼록 본 교재가 앞으로 계속적으로 진행될 어휘 학습 과정의 실용적인 초석이 되기를 바랍니다.

CONTENTS

LESSON 1

THE VERB, HAVE

CONTENTS

—

QUESTION OF THE DAY

Jennifer: *Hello, students of HYCU. My name is Jennifer. It's very nice to meet you! In this class, I'm going to help you study English vocabulary. How? Well, I'm going to ask you some questions. And you can just answer them in English! Don't worry about your English. You can practice it with me! OK. Here's my first question. Please try to answer it in English.* 매일 아침식사를 하시나요? *How would you say this in English?*

....

READ AND UNDERSTAND

Jennifer: *Now please read the following with me and answer my questions.*

> I usually **have breakfast** every morning. To be healthy, it's very important for us to eat breakfast. But sometimes, I **have a big breakfast**, and I eat it very quickly. So that's not good. Once, I got a stomachache! I also don't skip lunch. I usually eat out with my colleagues. Then I take a short rest. I search the Internet and read the news. During this time, I enjoy **having black tea** with honey. For dinner, I cook and eat at home. I try to **have a small dinner** because it is not good to **have a big meal** at night.

1. Do I usually eat breakfast every morning?

   ....

2. In my office, do I rest for a long time or a short time?

   ....

3. Which tea do I like to drink?

   ....

A. WordStudy : Have

Have = own / possess

- I **have** a laptop.
- I **have** a smart phone.

Have = hold, take part in

- At (my) work, we **have** a meeting every Monday.
- My company **has** a yearly picnic for the employees.

Have = eat / drink food

- I **have** breakfast every morning.
- Can I **have** a cup of coffee / tea with you?

Have = sick (with a disease)

- Don't come close to me. I **have** a cold.
- I **have** a stomachache. I also **have** indigestion.
- I **have** a headache. I **have** a fever, too.

Have = take classes

(Prof. to Student)

A: How many classes do you **have** this semester?

B: I **have** three classes.

B. Idioms / Proverbs

Try to guess the meaning of each idiom or proverb before you watch the lecture.

- tell a secret easily [입이 가볍다, 싸다]
- like sweet flavor too much [단것, 음식을 좋아하다]
- be (romantically) interested in somebody (only)
  [(오직) …만을 바라보다, 사랑하다]
- be out of touch with the outside world, that is, be unrealistic or naive
  [현실적이지 않다, 터무니없는 생각을 하다, 공상하다]
- be good at finding or recognizing something
  […을 알아보는, 찾아내는 능력이 있다]

Have one's head in the clouds

1. He has never been in business, but he thinks he can do well once he starts his own. He **has his head in the clouds**.

   = ...

Have eyes (only) for somebody

2. If I marry someone, I will **have eyes for** my husband / wife only.

   = ...

Have a nose for something*

3. The woman **has an amazing nose for** a bargain.

   = ...

* 또는 have a knack for something

Have a big mouth

4. Don't trust her too much. She **has a big mouth**.

   = ...

Have a sweet tooth

5. I really can't resist all those good desserts. I think I **have a sweet tooth**.

   = ...

C. Phrasal Verbs : Have ... on

Try to guess the meaning of each phrasal verb before you watch the lecture.

> (Mother to Daughter)
> A : You got all wet!
> B : Yeah, I didn't **have a raincoat on**.

1. "Have something on" means : ....

> (Between Friends)
> A : Oh, look at you in this photo. You **had dark eye shadow on**.
> B : Don't you remember? That was in fashion in those days.

2. "Have something on" means : ....

D. This is Confusing!

철수: 교수님, Oh, you **have to** be extremely tired! 의 의미가 '너는 몹시 피곤**해야만** 한다'인가요?

교수님: 좋은 질문입니다. 그럼 잘 들어보세요!

Have to = Requirement

You **have to** pass the exam if you want to graduate.

Have to = Guessing with Near Certainty

A: I worked the night shift last night.

B: Oh, you **have to** be extremely tired!

E. Variety / Register / Nuance: Have to vs. Must

For Requirement

Less Common:

You **must** pass the exam if you want to graduate.

More Common:

You **have to** pass the exam if you want to graduate.

For Guessing with Near Certainty

Less Common:

A: I worked the night shift last night.

B: Oh, you **have to** be extremely tired!

More Common:

A: I worked the night shift last night.

B: Oh, you **must** be extremely tired!

F. Word Parts: Prefixes (un-/dis-)

Un-/Dis- + Base Word = Negative/Opposite Meaning

Un- + Happy (Adj.)	=	Unhappy (Adj.)
Dis- + Like (V)	=	Dislike (V)
Dis- + Advantage (N)	=	Disadvantage (N)

- The man looked very nice, but actually he was very unkind.
- He was watching TV with me, but when I went out to get some fresh air, he just disappeared.

Guess the meaning of each underlined word. Follow the three steps.

1. The report discloses that the accident was due to human error.

   Step 1: Disclose = ... + ...

   Step 2: Base Word Meaning = ...

   Step 3: New Word Meaning = ...

2. There are many unemployed college graduates in Korea. We need more jobs to help them.

   Step 1: Unemployed = ...

   Step 2: Unemployed = ... + ...

   Step 3: Base Word Meaning = ...

Jennifer: *Hello again. Are you following the lesson well? It's time for me to check your understanding! You and I will have a mini conversation. In each conversation, I will be a pharmacist, dentist, or your friend. Let's begin!*

1. **상황: 약사와의 대화 – 감기약을 사러 약국에 들름**

Pharmacist: Good morning. (안녕하세요.)
You: .... (안녕하세요.)
Pharmacist: What can I do for you today? (무엇을 도와드릴까요?)
You: .... (감기에 걸렸어요.)
Pharmacist: Oh, I'm sorry. Are you coughing and sneezing?
(오, 저런! 기침도 하고 재채기도 하나요?)
You: .... (네.)

2. **상황: 치과의사와의 대화 – 검진을 받으러 치과에 들름**

Dentist: Let's see. Hmm, you have lots of tooth decay.
(자, 봅시다. 충치가 많군요.)
You: I knew that. (그럴 줄 알았어요.)
....
(제가 단것을 많이 좋아하거든요.)
Dentist: Hmm. You'd better eat less sugar.
(앞으로 단것은 적게 먹는 것이 좋겠어요.)
You: .... (네, 앞으로 그러도록 노력할게요.)

3. **상황: 친구와의 대화 – 줄에서 기다리는 중 앞 여성에 대해 귓속말을 함**

Friend: Do you smell something, too? (무슨 냄새 나지 않아?)
You: .... (응. 무슨 냄새지?)
Friend: I think that's perfume. (향수 같아.)
You: Wow, ...
(굉장히 강한 향수를 뿌렸나 봐.)

Jennifer: *On this last page, you'll do a final review of today's lesson. I'll read aloud five Korean sentences. Please express them in English, OK? Write sentences and check the example sentences.*

1. **저희 직장에서는 수요일마다 회의를 합니다.**

....

2. **(친구에게) 맥주 한잔 해.** (= 맥주 한잔 하지 그래?)

....

3. **(약사에게) 두통이 있고, 열도 나요.**

....

4. **(선생님이 학생에게) 너 또 공상에 빠져 있구나!**

....

5. **그녀는 입이 싼 편이에요.**

....

LESSON 2

THE VERB, TAKE

CONTENTS

QUESTION OF THE DAY

Jennifer: *Students, how are you today? Are you having a great day? I hope so. Well, it's time for you to answer my question! If somebody says, "I have a cold," what would you say? In Korea, you might say, 약은 좀 드셨나요? How would you say this in English?*

....

READ AND UNDERSTAND

Jennifer: *Now please read the following with me and answer my questions.*

> This morning, I woke up at 7 o' clock. As usual, I **took a walk** for about an hour. Then I **took a shower**. I had a big breakfast after that. At around 10 am, I left home and **took a taxi**. I usually **take the subway** to work but today was very cold. When I got to my office at Hanyang Cyber University, I had a cup of coffee and did some work for Prof. Park. Maybe because I had a big breakfast, I didn't feel hungry for lunch. So I continued to work till 6 pm then left for home. It was a long day, but I wasn't tired at all. I think I like teaching!

1. This morning, how long did I walk?

   ....

2. Why did I take a taxi today?

   ....

3. Did I have lunch today?

   ....

A. Word Study : Take

Take = transportation

A: How do you get to work?

B: I **take** the bus / the subway / the train / a taxi.

Compare
- I drive (my car).
- I ride my bicycle / my motorcycle.

- I take my car.
- I take my bicycle / my motorcycle.

Take = time (it + take(s) + (somebody) + time)

A: How long does it **take** to get to work?

B: It **takes** (me) an hour to get to work. / One hour.

A: How long does it **take** to eat lunch?

B: It **takes** (me) about 20 minutes to eat my lunch.
/ About 20 minutes.

Take = classes / lessons / a course, an exam / a test

A: Do you have a lot of exams this semester?

B: Yeah, because I'm **taking** seven classes!

- I want to **take** an acoustic guitar lesson.
- I'm going to **take** a cooking class this month.

A: What do you have to do to graduate?

B: In our department, we have to **take** a graduation exam.

Take = medicine

A: I have a cold.

B: Did you **take** medicine?

Compare Did you eat medicine? (X)

- I **take** a vitamin pill every day.

Compare I eat a vitamin pill every day. (X)

Take = pictures / photos, a shower / a bath, a nap / a break

- Could you please **take** a picture of us?
- Wow! Look at this beautiful photo! Who **took** it?

- In the summer, I **take** a shower twice a day.
- I like to **take** a hot bath once a week.

- You shouldn't **take** a nap right after a meal.
- Let's **take** a break. Do you want a cup of coffee?

Take = take something (with you)

(In the morning)

- **Take** an umbrella (with you). It might rain today.

Take = take somebody (to some place)

- Yesterday, I **took** my girlfriend **to** a restaurant to propose to her.

A: Do you know where Hanyang Cyber University is?

B: I can **take** you there. I'm on my way there, too.

B. Idioms / Proverbs

Try to guess the meaning of each idiom or proverb before you watch the lecture.

- Something else is more important. [부차적인 것이 되다, 중요하지 않게 되다]
- unpleasant at first, but becomes better with time
  [익숙해지려면 시간이 걸린다]
- Both people are responsible, not just one person.
  [손바닥도 마주쳐야 소리가 난다, 양쪽에 책임이 있다]
- do not hate something but do not particularly like it, either
  [그렇게 좋아하지도 싫어하지도 않다, 해도 그만 안 해도 그만]
- do not value somebody/something because this person/thing is always there […을 당연시하다, …이 고마운 줄을 모르다]

It takes two to tango.

1. A: Mom, Jill's always arguing with me!
   B: Well, **it takes two to tango**.

   = ...

(Somebody/something) take a back seat

2. A: How're your studies going?
   B: Unfortunately, **they're taking a back seat**. I have a big project to do at work.

   = ...

I can take it or leave it.

3. My sister loves pizza and pasta. But for me, **I can take it or leave it**. I love Korean food.

   = ...

Take somebody / something for granted

4. Don't **take your wife for granted** because she's always there for you.

   = ...

It takes (some) getting used to.

5. If Kimchi is new to you, **it might take some getting used to**. But it's worth it. Eventually most people like Kimchi.

   = ...

C. Phrasal Verbs: Take ... off / Take off ...

Try to guess the meaning of each phrasal verb before you watch the lecture.

> (Wife to Husband)
>
> A: It's so hot today. Jessie must be hot, too. Honey, could you **take her jacket off**?
>
> B: Sure.

1. "Take something off / Take off something" means: ....

(Korean Friend to American Friend)

A: Could you **take off your shoes** before you come in?

B: May I ask you why?

A: Oh, it's just our way of living in Korea.

2. "Take something off/Take off something" means: ....

(Daughter to Mother)

A: Mom, I'm so tired today. I might not be able to go to work tomorrow.

B: Why don't you **take a day off** and sleep in, sweetheart?

3. "Take a day (time) off" means: ....

D. This is Confusing!

철수: 교수님, Take off **her jacket** 대신에 Take off **it**을 사용해도 되나요? 즉 take off와 같은 구동사 뒤에 대명사가 위치해도 되는지 궁금해요.

교수님: 좋은 질문입니다. 그럼 잘 들어보세요!

(Child Calling Mom on the Phone)

A: Hello?

B: Mom, Jessie's sick! She has a fever and is sweating!

A: OK, honey. Calm down. First, take off **her jacket!** (OK)

B: I took off **it**, mom. (NOT OK)
Now what do I do?

OK	*NOT OK*
I took **her jacket** off.	
I took off **her jacket**.	
I took **it** off.	I took off **it**.

E. Variety / Register / Nuance : Take vs. Have

Common for American English

A: The weather's nice.
B: Yeah, let's **take** a walk.
(Take a shower / a bath / a rest / a swim / a walk / a look / a listen)

Common for British English

A: The weather's nice.
B: Yes, let's **have** a walk.
(Have a shower / a bath / a rest / a swim / a walk / a look / a listen)

F. Word Parts: Prefixes (mis- / non-)

Mis- / Non- + Base Word
= Something Done Badly or Not Well / Not Something

Mis- + behave (V)	=	Misbehave (V)
Mis- + understand (V)	=	Misunderstand (V)
Non- + smoking (Adj.)	=	Nonsmoking (Adj.)

- Some children do not misbehave when their parents are around.
- Would you like the smoking or the nonsmoking section?

Guess the meaning of each underlined word. Follow the three steps.

1. Only native speakers of English can teach English well? Most people would disagree. <u>Nonnative</u> speakers can also be good English teachers.

Step 1 : Nonnative = ... + ...
Step 2 : Base Word Meaning = ...
Step 3 : New Word Meaning = ...

2. (In a Workplace) I thought I understood his faxed order correctly, but I <u>misinterpreted</u> it.

Step 1 : Misinterpret = ...
Step 2 : Misinterpret = ... + ...
Step 3 : Base Word Meaning = ...

Jennifer: *Hey guys, welcome back! How're you doing in this lesson? Having fun, or are you bored? Well, it's time to help you speak! I'll be your conversation partner again. Let's begin!*

1. 상황: 이웃과의 대화 – 어떻게 출근하는지에 대해 이야기를 나눔

Neighbor: How do you get to work? (출근은 어떻게 하시나요?)
You: .... (지하철 타고 해요.)
Neighbor: How long does it take? (얼마나 걸려요?)
You: .... (30분 정도 걸려요.)

2. 상황: 친구와의 대화 – 주말을 어떻게 보낼지에 대해 이야기함

Friend: I'm going to spend time with my family this weekend. What about you? (이번 주말에 가족들과 시간을 보낼 계획인데, 넌 어때?)
You: ....
(글쎄, 요즘 가족들에게 신경을 못 쓰고 있어. 더 중요한 게 있어서 말이야.)
Friend: What's the matter? (무슨 일이라도 있어?)
You: ....
(이번 주말에 중간고사 시험을 쳐야 하거든.)
Friend: Oh, I'm sorry about that! (에구, 안됐구먼.)

3. 상황: 친구와의 대화 – 항상 피곤해 보이는 친구에게 한 가지 제안을 함

You: When I see you these days, you always look tired.
(요즘 너 볼 때마다 항상 피곤해 보이는 것 같아.)
Friend: I am very tired. I just have too much work – school and business. (사실 많이 피곤해. 할 일이 너무 많거든. 학교 공부며 일이며.)
You: ....
(이번 학기는 휴학을 해보지 그래?)
Friend: I might do that, but I want to think about it more.
(그럴지도 몰라. 그런데 더 생각해보고 결정하고 싶어.)

Jennifer: *On this last page, you'll do a final review of today's lesson. I'll read aloud five Korean sentences. Please express them in English, OK? Write sentences and check the example sentences.*

1. **이번 학기에 저는 수업 4개를 듣고 있어요.**

   ....

2. **(심한 감기에 걸린 상황) 저는 요즘 감기약(cold medicine)을 먹고 있어요.**

   ....

3. **좀 쉬었다 하자. 커피 한 잔 마실까?**

   ....

4. **좀 더 두터운 재킷 하나 가져가.**

   ....

5. **(저희) 사진 좀 찍어 주시겠어요?**

   ....

LESSON 3

THE VERBS, GO & COME

CONTENTS

—

QUESTION OF THE DAY

Jennifer: *Good morning! No? Then good afternoon? Yes and no? I see. Some people study in the early morning. Some people study at night. Right? So everyone studies! Great! OK. Are you guys ready? Today's question is* (당신) 사무실에 가도 될까요? *How would you say this in English?*

....

LISTEN AND UNDERSTAND

Jennifer: *Now please listen to the following and answer my questions.*

(Jennifer and Mike Talking on the Phone)

Mike: I hear you had a lot of fun last Sunday!

Jennifer: Yeah! I **went to Insadong**. I saw a lot of stores there!

Mike: Did you **go into any of them**?

Jennifer: Sure. And I got some interesting stuff.

Mike: I want to take a look at it. Can I **come to your place** sometime… today?

Jennifer: Sure. You can **come to my place** any time today.

Mike: Great! I'll call you before I **go**.

1. I went to Insadong today. *True* *False*

2. Mike will come to my place today. *True* *False*

3. I did not go into any stores in Insadong. *True* *False*

A. Word Study : Go & Come

Go = moving from place A to place B

- Every day, I **go** to the gym before work.
- Last year, I **went** to China.

Go = leave a place to do an activity

- Why don't we **go** shopp**ing** after lunch?

A: Where're the kids?
B: They **went** swimm**ing**/karaoke sing**ing**.

Go = change of state, become (usu. followed by adjectives)

A: Dad's **go**ing bald.
B: Well, not surprising. Granddad's bald, you know.

(hair, person) **go grey** (soup) **go bad** (person) **go mad**

Go = transportation/directions

- Does this bus **go** downtown?
- Which subway **goes** to Hanyang Cyber University?

Go = where something is supposed to be, the usual place to be

A: Where do these dishes **go**?
B: { You can put them in / They **go** into } the second cabinet. Thanks.

Go = future plans, be going to V

- Tomorrow I'**m going to** go shopping for my sister. This Saturday is her birthday.
- (Teacher to Student) When **are** you **going to** take the quiz? The due date is coming up.

Come = move towards the speaker / listener

- To a dog : Hey, **come** here.
- I'll **come** to your place this evening.

Come = come for something / to do something

- (At a clothing repair shop / At a tailor's shop) I've **come** for my pants. Are they ready?
- (A repairman visiting the house) I've **come** to check your Internet connection.

Come = take a certain position

- I **came** first in the 100-meter sprint!
- I **came** second in the midterm exam!

Come = come in a certain state

- These pants **come** in three colors : black, navy, and grey.
- Imported cars don't **come** cheap.

Come = happen (to ask about a reason or how in a question)

- How did you **come to** break your arms?
- (Friend to Friend)

  A: I'm leaving class early today.

  B: **How come?** (= Why?)

B. Idioms / Proverbs

Try to guess the meaning of each idiom or proverb before you watch the lecture.

- be very successful [크게 성공하다]
- make great progress [많이 발전하다, 진전을 보다]
- suddenly or immediately think of something [(문득) 생각, 기억나다]
- If a situation becomes very serious or difficult [최악의 경우에는]
- have known each other for many years [오랫동안 알고 지내다]
- can't think of anything [머리가 하얘지다, 아무 생각이 나지 않다]

Go a long way

1-1. I believe John will **go a long way**. He works very hard and does his best in everything.

= ....

Go back a long way

1-2. A: Congratulations on your marriage! How long have you known each other?

B: Well, we **go back a long way**. We first met in elementary school.

= ....

Come a long way

2. John has **come a long way**. When he entered HYCU, he wasn't able to say even a sentence in English. But now he can express himself very fluently.

   = ...

Come to mind

3. When I think of him, a lot of things immediately **come to mind**. We did a lot of crazy things together when we were young.

   = ...

Your mind goes blank.

4. When I saw the question on the exam, **my mind** immediately **went blank**. I had prayed and prayed so I wouldn't have to answer the question.

   = ...

If (the) worst comes to (the) worst

5. **If (the) worst comes to (the) worst**, I'll just sell my car and take the bus to work.

   = ...

C. Phrasal Verbs : Go on / Come on!

Try to guess the meaning of each phrasal verb before you watch the lecture.

(Husband to Wife in an Apartment Building)

A : Do you hear the noise above us, too?

B : Yeah. What's **going on** there? Are they having a fight or something?

1. "Go on" means : ....

(Friend to Friend)

A : How was the picnic?

B : You won't believe it! It **went on raining** all day! It didn't stop.

2. "Go on V-ing" means : ....

(Husband to Wife at Home)

A : **Come on**, honey! We really need to go now.

B : Just wait another minute. I'm not ready.

A : You look great! Let's go now.

3. "Come on" means : ....

(Friend to Friend at a Bar)

A : I think I'm getting drunk. I should stop now.

B : Oh, **come on!** Have another drink. You look fine!

A : If I drink more, my wife won't open the door for me!

4. "Come on" means : ....

D. This is Confusing

철수: 교수님, '어떻게 지내세요?'라고 할 때 How's it **going**? 이라고 하잖아요. 그러면 How's it **coming**? 도 같은 의미로 쓸 수 있을까요?

교수님: 좋은 질문입니다. 그럼 잘 들어보세요!

To Mean "How are you (doing)?"

(Colleague to Colleague at Work)

A: **How's it going**, John? (OK) → **How's it coming**, John? (NOT OK)

B: Pretty good. How about you?

To Ask about a Particular Subject

A: **How's your project going / coming (along)**, John? (OK)

B: It's going well. / It's coming along well. Thanks for asking!

A: I hear you started **a new project**.

B: Yeah, I did.

A: **How's it going / coming (along)**? (OK)

E. Variety / Register / Nuance: Going To vs. Gonna

Two Pronunciations to Express Future Plans Using "Going To"

Less Casual

Friend 1: What're you **going to** do tomorrow?

Friend 2: I'm **going to** go shopping for my sister.

More Casual

Friend 1: What're you **gonna** do tomorrow?

Friend 2: I'm **gonna** go shopping for my sister.

F. Word Parts: Prefixes (im- / il-)

Im- / Il- + Base Word = Opposite Meaning

Im- + Possible (Adj.)	=	Impossible (Adj.)
Il- + Legal (Adj.)	=	Illegal (Adj.)

- "Mission Impossible" means a very difficult or dangerous mission.
- Currently, euthanasia is illegal in Korea.

Guess the meaning of each underlined word. Follow the three steps.

1. In Korea, people hesitate to ask about someone's salary because it could be an impolite question.

   Step 1 : Impolite = ... + ...
   Step 2 : Base Word Meaning = ...
   Step 3 : New Word Meaning = ...

2. Today, most Koreans are literate. However, a long time ago, before King Sejong invented Hangul, a lot of them were illiterate. They could not read or write.

   Step 1 : Illiterate = ...
   Step 2 : Illiterate = ... + ...
   Step 3 : Base Word Meaning = ...

Jennifer: *Hi guys! How're you doing? It's time again for you to practice some of the words and expressions you've learned so far. Shall we start?*

1. **상황: 낯선 사람에게 시내로 가는 버스가 어떤 버스인지 묻고 있음**

You: Excuse me. (실례합니다.)
.... (버스 100번은 시내로 가나요?)
Stranger: No, it goes to the airport. (아니요, 그 버스는 공항으로 가요.)
You: Oh, OK. Then, which bus can take us downtown?
(그럼 어느 버스를 타야 저희가 시내로 갈 수 있나요?)
Stranger: Take 105. (105번을 타세요.)
You: .... (감사합니다!)
Stranger: No problem! (천만에요.)

2. **상황: 다른 업체 직원과 일 관계로 전화 통화 중**

Employee of Another Company: So, we should have another meeting.
(다시 회의를 하는 것이 좋겠네요.)
You: Sure. ....
(언제쯤 당신 사무실로 가면 될까요?)
Employee of Another Company: How about 2 pm? (오후 2시 어때요?)
You: Sounds good. (좋습니다.)

3. **상황: 교수님과의 대화 – 시험이 어땠는지에 대해 이야기를 나눔**

Professor: How did you feel about the exam? Do you think you did well? (시험은 어땠어요? 잘 봤어요?)
You: Sorry, professor. I didn't do well. (죄송해요, 교수님. 잘 못 봤어요.)
Professor: What happened? I know you studied hard!
(무슨 일 있었어요? 공부 열심히 했잖아요.)
You: Yes, but when I saw the first question on the exam (네, 열심히 했는데요, 첫 문제를 보는 순간), ...
(그냥 머릿속이 하얘졌어요!)

Jennifer: *On this last page, you'll do a final review of today's lesson. I'll read aloud five Korean sentences. Please express them in English, OK? Write sentences and check the example sentences.*

1. 나는 일요일에 등산(hike)하러 갈 계획이다.

   ....

2. (점원이 손님에게) 이 상품(product)은 두 가지 디자인으로 나옵니다.

   ....

3. 최악의 경우엔 피아노를 팔지 뭐.

   ....

4. 무슨 일이야?

   ....

5. 어제는 하루 종일 눈이 계속 내렸어.

   Yesterday, ...

LESSON 4

THE VERB, MAKE

CONTENTS

—

QUESTION OF THE DAY

Jennifer: *Hi everyone! How was your week? Did you do something fun? I hope you study and play as well! Remember "all work and no play makes Jack a dull boy." OK. Today's question is* 댁에서는 누가 저녁을 준비하나요? *How would you say this in English?*

....

READ AND UNDERSTAND

Jennifer: *Now please read the following with me and answer my questions.*

> Today I'll talk about my beautiful mother when she was younger. She was a very busy person. (She's still busy!) She ran her own business. She had a pizza restaurant. But she **made three meals** every school day for us! My sister and I always took lunch boxes to school. My mother was very good with her hands. She **made the clothes and dresses** for our dolls! She was also a very wise woman. When she had to **make a decision**, she took enough time. So she did not **make a lot of mistakes**.

1. My mother owned a pizza restaurant. ***True*** ***False***

2. She cooked three meals every school day. ***True*** ***False***

3. She made a lot of mistakes. ***True*** ***False***

A. Word Study : Make

Make = create / prepare / cook

- I sometimes **make** my own clothes.
- Go ahead and take a shower. I'll **make** coffee.
- I **make** dinner and my husband **makes** breakfast.

Make = a mess / a mistake / a scene

- My husband always **makes** a mess when he cooks.
- Try to be generous when other people **make** mistakes.
- Please don't **make** a scene in public. Let's talk about it at home.

Make = a decision / a choice / a guess / a comment / a suggestion / a phone call

- Don't **make** a quick decision. You need to take your time.
- It's a mystery. We can only **make** a guess about what really happened.
- He **made** some very helpful comments on my paper.

Make = a friend / an enemy

- As we get older, it gets more difficult to **make** good friends.
- Some people **make** a lot of enemies in their company.

Make = money / progress / a difference / changes

- One of my friends **makes** money by singing in cafes.
- I've **made** a lot of progress. I can introduce myself in English now!
- Studying at HYCU has **made** a big difference in my life.

Make = become (+ N)

- You love children and like teaching. You'll **make** a very good kindergarten teacher.

Make = cause (+ N / Pron + Adj) / cause (+ N / Pron + V) / cause (+ N / Pron + N)

- My marriage **made** my mom very happy.
- My mom always **makes** me laugh.
- All work and no play **makes** Jack a dull boy.

Make = force (+ N / Pron + V)

- My little brother always **makes** me read a book to him. Otherwise, he cries and never goes to sleep!

B. Idioms / Proverbs

Try to guess the meaning of each idiom or proverb before you watch the lecture.

- make a decision [결정하다]
- make you happy […을 매우 행복하게 해주다]
- become very good at something if you keep doing it [자꾸 연습하다 보면 잘하게 된다]
- If you want to be treated well, you should treat other people well, too. [자업자득, 뿌린 대로 거둔다]
- produce a certain look on your face to show that you do not like someone or something [얼굴을 찌푸리다, 일그러뜨리다]

Make your day

1. (Listener Talking on the Phone with a Radio Show Anchor)

A: I always listen to your show, and I really enjoy it. Your show makes me relax.

B: Oh, thank you. You've just **made my day**!

= ....

Make a face

2. John **made a face** when he saw spinach on his plate.

   = ...

Make up your mind

3. Both shirts are cool! I can't **make up my mind**!

   = ...

Practice makes perfect.

4. You want to speak English well? Then speak it every day. **Practice makes perfect**!

   = ...

A good husband makes a good wife.*

5. (Husband to his Friend)

   A: My wife and I are having a lot of fights these days.

   B: Remember, a good husband makes a good wife.

   = ...

* 또는 You reap what you sow. / What {comes / goes} around {goes / comes} around.

C. Phrasal Verbs : Make ... up ... / Make up (with someone)

Try to guess the meaning of each phrasal verb before you watch the lecture.

(Student to Professor)

A : Professor, I'm very sorry. I missed class yesterday. Can I **make it up**?

B : If you write a report on what we covered, you'll be okay.

1. "Make something up / Make up something" means : ....

(Friend to Friend)

A : When you fight with your wife, how do you **make up with her**?

B : I usually apologize first. Then we go out for a nice dinner.

2. "Make up (with someone)" means : ....

D. This is Confusing!

철수 : 교수님, 라디오에서 우연히 You can make it이란 말을 들었는데 제가 알고 있던 make의 의미가 아니었던 것 같아요. 혹시 **You can make it**이란 표현이 따로 있나요?

교수님 : 좋은 질문입니다. 그럼 잘 들어보세요!

To Achieve a Goal, Be Successful

(Friend to Friend)

A : I promised myself I'd stop smoking for six months and I have one month left. But I'm not sure if I can continue.

B : **You can make it!**

(Friend to Friend)

A: I've always dreamed of playing in an orchestra, but the competition is fierce. I feel like giving up.

B: **You can make it.** Don't give up!

To Create Something

(Friend to Friend)

A: Look at that beautiful cake! I wish **I could make that**!

B: Guess what? **I can make it**!

To Arrive at a Place That Has Been Arranged

(Friend to Friend)

A: Nice to see you again! I'm glad **you could make it**.

B: Thanks! { I'm happy to be here, too. / It's good to see you again, too. }

To Ask if Someone Can Come in Time

(Colleague to Colleague)

A: Since we have a lot to discuss, why don't we meet a little early this week?

B: Sure. What time should we meet?

A: How about 8am? **Can you make it**?

E. Variety / Register / Nuance
: (Make a) Mistake vs. Error

Casual Situations

Natural:

I **made the mistake** of giving him my cell phone number.

Awkward:

I **made the error** of giving him my cell phone number.

Serious Situations

Natural:

I **had made a grave error** in giving him my cell phone number. It turned out he was a convicted felon.

F. Word Parts: Prefixes (in- / ir-)

In- / Ir- + Base Word = Opposite Meaning

In- + Correct (Adj.)	=	Incorrect (Adj.)
Ir- + Regular (Adj.)	=	Irregular (Adj.)

- That's an <u>incorrect</u> answer. Can you try it again?
- I have <u>irregular</u> meals. I know it's not good for my health.

Guess the meaning of each underlined word. Follow the three steps.

1. When you write a business letter in English, try not to be <u>informal</u>. For instance, avoid using "don't." Write "do not."

   Step 1 : Informal = ...

   Step 2 : Informal = ... + ...

   Step 3 : Base Word Meaning = ...

2. Some young parents are very <u>irresponsible</u>. They are only interested in online games, so they forget to take care of their babies.

   Step 1 : Irresponsible = ...

   Step 2 : Irresponsible = ... + ...

   Step 3 : Base Word Meaning = ...

Jennifer: *Hi guys! How're you doing? It's time again for you to practice some of the words and expressions you've learned so far. Shall we start?*

1. **상황: 배우자에게 집안일을 공평하게 분담하자고 이야기하는 중**

You: We both work. So we need to share the housework.
(우리는 둘 다 일하니까 집안일을 좀 나눠야겠어요.)
Spouse: Fair. For meals, I'll make breakfast and coffee.
(맞는 말이에요. 식사는…… 제가 아침과 커피를 만들게요.)
You: Then, ...
(그럼 제가 저녁과 차를 만들게요.)
Spouse: Perfect! (좋아요!)

2. **상황: (무서운!) 엄마가 자식을 야단치고 있는 중**

You: .... (인상 풀어!)
Child: (Still holding an angry expression)
(여전히 화가 난 표정)
You: It's your fault. You pulled your sister's hair.
(그건 네가 잘못한 거야. 언니 머리카락을 잡아당겼잖아.)
....
(언니한테 사과해. 지금!)

3. **상황: 대신 야근을 해준 직장 동료에게 고맙다는 인사를 하는 중**

You: ....
(야근 대신 해줘서 고마워요!)
Co-worker: Sure. (별말씀을요.)
You: ....
(어떻게 하면 제가 보답할 수 있을까요?)
Co-worker: Well, you can just do the same for me when I need your help. (그냥 제가 도움이 필요하면 똑같이 해주세요.)

Jennifer: *On this last page, you'll do a final review of today's lesson. I'll read aloud five Korean sentences. Please express them in English, OK? Write sentences and check the example sentences.*

1. **(어머니가 자녀에게) (애기가 자고 있으니까) 시끄럽게 하지 마. 알았지?**

   ....

2. **내 아이들을 보면 난 항상 미소 짓게 된다. (= 내 아이들은 항상 나를 미소 짓게 한다.)**

   ....

3. **두 개 다 좋아서 못 고르겠어 (= 결정할 수가 없어.)**

   ....

4. **차를 살 때는 신중히 결정하는 것이 좋다.**

   When we buy a car, ...

5. **집 한 채를 살려면 돈을 더 벌어야 한다.**

   In order to buy a house, I need to ....

LESSON 5

THE VERB, DO

CONTENTS

—

QUESTION OF THE DAY

Jennifer: *Hi, guys! How was your weekend? You watched our lesson? I hope you learned a lot! Well, let's get started. As usual, I'm going to ask a question and you'll answer in English. What do you do? What's your job?*

....

READ AND UNDERSTAND

Jennifer: *Now please read the following with me and answer my questions.*

> You know I take a walk every morning. I **do this** to keep healthy. But I also **do other things** for exercise. I'll talk about these today. Every Saturday, I do yoga for an hour. Then I go biking along the Han River. I feel very fresh and light! And I also get exercise when I **do the housework**. For instance, when I **do the dishes**, I stand on my toes. At first, it was difficult, but then it got easier. Finally, I **do wall-climbing**. I don't **do this** often, but when I am stressed, I **do wall-climbing**. While I'm **doing this sport**, I forget about my worries.

1. How often do I do yoga?

....

2 What do I do along the Han River?

....

3. Why do I do wall-climbing?

....

A. Word Study : Do

Do = action

- What are they **do**ing over there?
- What can I **do** for you today? (= How may/can I help you?)

Do = task / activity

- I always **did** (my) homework before I went out to play.
- I **did** some research on this topic.
- I **do** a lot of business with the US.

- I hate **do**ing the dishes / the laundry (the wash) / the housework.
- I love **do**ing the cooking / the cleaning.

- I **did** a little acting / writing / singing when I was in college.

- I **do** yoga / wall-climbing every weekend.

Do = job

A: What do you **do** (for a living)? (= What's your job?)
B: I'm a student / a professor.

Do = how someone is / succeed

- How (are) you **do**ing?
- How's your family **do**ing?

A: How was your exam?
B: I didn't **do** a good job / I didn't **do** well / I **did** { badly. / poorly }

A: How's your business **do**ing?

B: It's **do**ing well.

Do = study a particular subject

A: What's your major?

B: I'm **do**ing a double major — English and Counseling.

I **did** English and German in high school.

Do = make / produce / provide a service

A: Does this restaurant **do** an early breakfast?

B: Sorry, we don't open until 9 am.

Do = cook

(Waiter to Guest)

A: How would you like your steak (**done**)?

B: Well-**done**, please.

Do you know how to **do** Bulgogi?

Do = finish

(Parent to Child)

A: Did you finish/**do** your homework?

B: Yep! { Just **done**! / Almost **done**! }

B. Idioms / Proverbs

Try to guess the meaning of each idiom or proverb before you watch the lecture.

- Make sure you have some alternatives.
  [한 가지 일에 모든 걸 걸지 마라, 대안을 가져라]
- It is not easy to earn/get money.
  [돈은 그리 쉽게 생기는 것이 아니다, 땅을 파도 10원 한 장 안 나온다]
- Don't be so sure about the results of something. Wait until it actually happens.
  [김칫국부터 마시지 마라]
- do what I want to do without following other people's ideas
  [(다른 사람의 시선, 생각과 상관없이) …가 하고 싶은 대로 하다]
- People need more than physical things such as food, houses, and money.
  [사람은 빵만으로는 살 수 없다, 물질이 다가 아니다]

Do your own thing.

1. My parents want me to be a lawyer, but I like drawing. I'm going to **do my own thing**.

   = ...

Money does not grow on trees.

2. He spends money too easily. He should realize **money doesn't grow on trees**.

   = ...

Man does not live by bread alone.*

3. A: Mr. Rich killed himself! He had a lot of money and fame.
   B: You know, **man does not live by bread alone**.

   = ...

Don't count your chickens before they hatch.

4. (Playing Online Games)
   Don't count your chickens before they hatch. The game isn't over!

   = ...

Don't put all your eggs in one basket.

5. A: I've applied for a lot of positions. Hopefully, I'll get hired for one of them.
   B: That's a good idea. "**Don't put all your eggs in one basket**."

   = ...

* 또는 It takes more than money to be happy.

C. Phrasal Verbs : Do ... over / Do away with ...

Try to guess the meaning of each phrasal verb before you watch the lecture.

(Student to Professor)

A : Professor, I got a bad grade on my paper. Can I **do it over**?

B : Unfortunately, no. Everyone gets just one chance.

1. "Do something over" means : ....

(Street Reporter to Citizen)

A : Excuse me, ma'am! I'm doing a survey about opinions. What should we **do away with** in society?

B : I believe, stereotypes. People need fair chances.

2. "Do away with something" means : ....

D. This is Confusing!

철수 : 교수님, 어떻게 지내냐고 인사할 때 How's it going?은 가능하지만, How's it coming?은 가능하지 않다고 하셨잖아요. 그럼 **How's it doing?** 이란 표현은 어떤가요??

교수님 : 좋은 질문입니다. 그럼 잘 들어보세요!

To Mean "How are you (doing)?"

(Friends' Greeting)

A: How's it going? (OK)

→ **How's it doing?** (NOT OK)

→ **How's it coming (along)?** (NOT OK)

B: Pretty good. Thanks. Yourself?

To Ask about a Particular Subject

A: I hear you opened **a restaurant**.

B: Yeah. A week ago.

A: How's **it** going/**do**ing/coming (along)? (OK)

B: For now, it's going/**do**ing/coming along very well. (OK)

E. Variety / Register / Nuance
: Do you have vs. Have you got

Common in Spoken American English

- **Do you have** a car?
- I **have** a car. / I'**ve got** a car.
- She **has** a car. / She'**s got** a car.
- She **doesn't have** a car.
- They **don't have** a car.

Common in Spoken British English

- **Have you got** a car?
- I'**ve got** a car. (= I **have got** a car.)
- She'**s got** a car. (= She **has got** a car.)
- She **hasn't got** a car. (= She **has not got** a car.)
- They **haven't got** a car. (= They **have not got** a car.)

F. Word Parts: Prefixes (re- / over-)

Re- / Over- + Base Word = Again / Too Much

Re- + Do (V)	=	Redo (V)
Over- + Do (V)	=	Overdo (V)

- Professor, can I redo my paper? I can do better this time!
- Don't overdo it on your exercising. It can damage your health.

Guess the meaning of each underlined word. Follow the three steps.

1. The walls of the room were painted a year ago, but I need to repaint them.

Step 1 : Repaint = ... + ...

Step 2 : Base Word Meaning = ...

Step 3 : New Word Meaning = ...

2. She has a lot of work experience in this field. But her new position is very low. I think she is overqualified.

Step 1 : Overqualified = ...

Step 2 : Overqualified = ... + ...

Step 3 : Base Word Meaning = ...

Jennifer: *It's time to do some role play with Jennifer! Are you ready? I'm ready! Let's go!*

1. **상황: 한양사이버대학교 오프라인 모임에서 처음으로 만난 학우들의 대화**

You: ....
(어떤 일을 하고 계십니까?)
Another Student: I have my own business. (제 개인 사업을 하고 있어요.)
You: Oh, cool! What business do you have?
(멋진데요! 어떤 사업인데요?)
Another Student: I run a private educational institute.
(학원을 운영하고 있습니다.)

2. **상황: 집안일을 돕지 않는다고 엄마에게 혼이 난 친구가 다른 친구는 집에서 어떻게 하는지 물어보고 있는 중**

Friend: Do you help your mom?
(너 어머니 좀 거들어드리니?)
You: Well, I don't do much. (그다지 많이 하지는 않아.)
But ....
(그래도 모든 식사의 설거지는 내가 해.)
Friend: What about your dad? (너희 아버지는 뭘 하시고?)
You: He vacuums the carpet and takes out the trash.
(카펫을 진공청소기로 돌리시고 쓰레기를 버리셔.)

3. **상황: 아이가 돈을 쉽게 써버려서 나무라고 있는 중**

Child: Mom, can you give me 10,000 won? (엄마, 만 원만.)
You: I gave you 10,000 won two days ago. Did you spend it already?
(이틀 전에 만 원 줬잖아. 벌써 다 썼니?)
Child: (Silence)
You: Honey, ...
(얘야, 돈은 거저 생기는 게 아니란다.)

Jennifer: *On this last page, you'll do a final review of today's lesson. I'll read aloud five Korean sentences. Please express them in English, OK? Write sentences and check the example sentences.*

1. **시험 잘 봤어?**

   .... on the exam?

2. **사업은 어떻게 잘 되고 있어요?**

   ....

3. **저는 설거지하는 게 너무 싫어요!**

   ....

4. **이 브랜드는 스포츠웨어(sportswear)만 만드나요?**

   ....

5. **인간은 물질적인 것만으로는 살 수 없다.**

   ....

LESSON 6

THE VERB, GIVE

CONTENTS

—

QUESTION OF THE DAY

Jennifer: *Hello, students! How's it going with you all? Did you smile a lot over the past few days? Smiling is good for your health, so try to smile a lot! So, here's the question for the day.* 활짝 미소 지어봐! *How would you say this in English?*

....

LISTEN AND UNDERSTAND

Jennifer: *Now please listen to the following and answer my questions.*

Jennifer :	This Saturday I'm going to Gangnam to hang out with some students.
Mike :	Ah, hanging out Gangnam Style!
Jennifer :	Yeah, Gangnam Style.
Mike :	Actually, I have to meet a friend at 5:00 in Gangnam.
Jennifer :	Oh really? My meeting's at 5:00, too.
Mike :	Great! I can **give you a ride**.
Jennifer :	Thanks! And can you **give me a call** before you leave home?

1. Mike and I know the song, Gangnam Style. ***True*** ***False***

2. Mike will drive his car, and I will ride with him. ***True*** ***False***

3. I will call Mike before I leave. ***True*** ***False***

A. Word Study : Give

Give someone something = Give something to someone

Give = put something in someone's hands

(Between Sisters)

Did you **give** the mail to mom? = Did you give mom the mail?

Give = a present / money

(Sister Having Birthday Yesterday)

I **gave** a movie ticket to my sister. = I **gave** my sister a movie ticket.

Give = information / advice / time

(Talking with a Customer on the Phone)

Could you **give** me your (e-mail) address, please?

(Student to Professor)

Could you **give** me some advice on this matter?

= Could you advise me on this matter?

(Dad to Child about to Leave Home)

We don't have enough time. I'll **give** you 3 minutes. Hurry up!

Give = physical actions (give someone N)

He **gave** me a smile / a hug / a kiss / a frown.

= He smiled at / hugged / kissed / frowned at me.

(Friend Leaving a Message on the Answering Machine)

Can you **give** me a call when you get back?

= Can you call me when you get back?

(Child to Parent)

Can you **give** me some help with my homework?

= Can you help me with my homework?

(Friend to Friend)

Can you **give** me a ride (home)? = Can I ride in your car with you?

Give = a talk / a speech / a performance

- The professor will **give** a talk on Renaissance art this Saturday.
- He **gave** one of the best speeches of the 20th century.
- The new band will **give** its debut performance today.

Give = make someone sick / troubled

- Don't come too close to me. I don't want to **give** you my cold.

Give = pay / donate (+money)

- He **gave** me $200 for my old handbag.
- I **gave** $20 to the Salvation Army to help the poor.

Give = punish

- Surprisingly, the judge **gave** him 3 years in prison.

Give = grade exams / assignments

- The professor **gave** me a B+.

B. Idioms / Proverbs

Try to guess the meaning of each idiom or proverb before you watch the lecture.

- help someone […을 거들다, 도와주다]
- bother someone, make someone suffer […을 힘들게 하다, …의 애를 먹이다]
- decide to believe someone although s/he still has doubt [속는 셈 치고 믿어주다]
- give a yes sign so someone can start something […에게 승인을 해주다, 허락을 하다]
- willing to give something to others and to receive something from others [주고 받는 것, 상대방에 대한 서로의 양보]

Give and take

1. Marriage is about **give and take**. You can't give all the time. You should have something in return.

   = ...

Give someone a hand

2. (Man Saw Older Woman with Big Suitcase on Subway Stairs.)
   A: Ma'am! I can **give you a hand**!
   B: Oh, thank you very much!

   = ...

Give someone a hard/rough time

3. Three years ago, I forgot our wedding anniversary. But my wife is still **giving me a hard time** about it.

   = ...

Give someone / something the green light

4. A: How's your project going?

   B: Well, my boss hasn't **given me the green light** yet.

   = ...

Give someone the benefit of the doubt

5. (Parents Talking about their Child)

   A: Do you think she's telling the truth?

   B: I have no idea. Why don't you **give her the benefit of the doubt**?

   = ...

C. Phrasal Verbs: Give up (...) / Give (...) up

Try to guess the meaning of each phrasal verb before you watch the lecture.

> (Friends Talking about Movie)
>
> A: Have you seen the movie, "Titanic"?
>
> B: Of course. I can't forget their lines. When Rose said, "I love you, Jack," he said, "Don't say your goodbyes. Don't **give up**. Don't do it."

1. "Give up" means: ....

> (Colleague to Colleague at Work)
>
> A: How did you **give up** smok**ing**?
>
> B: Well, I just wanted to live longer… with my wife and two children.

2. "Give up something / Give something up" means: ....

D. This is Confusing!

철수: 교수님, Give 동사는 두 가지 문장구조가 가능하다고 배웠는데요. Give something to someone, 그리고 Give someone something! 그런데 Give someone something 구조에서 something 자리에 **대명사 it**을 쓰면, 즉 Give someone **it**처럼 쓰면 역시나 문법에 맞지 않는 문장이 되겠죠? 2차시에서 배운 Take off **it**과 비슷한 원리가 아닌가 생각돼요.

교수님: 좋은 질문입니다. 그럼 잘 들어보세요!

Give Something to Someone

A: Where's my flower vase?

B: Remember? We gave **it** to Jane. (OK)

Give Someone Something

A: Where's my flower vase?

B: Remember? We gave Jane **it**. (NOT OK)

E. Variety / Register / Nuance: Hug me. vs. Give me a hug.

In Spoken English

Less Common	*More Common*
Hug me.	Give me a hug.
Smile for me.	Give me a smile.
Advise me.	Give me some advice.

(Dad to Child Leaving Home)

A: I'll miss you a lot!

B: I'll miss you, too, Dad.

A: **Give me a hug**!

F. Word Parts: Prefixes (ex- / pre-)

Ex- / Pre- + Base Word = Was / Before

Ex- + Boyfriend (N)	=	Ex-boyfriend (N)
Pre- + School (N)	=	Preschool (N)

- I saw your ex-boyfriend the other day. He was with a new girl.
- My son goes to preschool. He'll go to kindergarten next year.

Guess the meaning of each underlined word. Follow the three steps.

1. My ex-wife and I worked at the same company before we got divorced.

   Step 1 : Ex-wife = ... + ...
   Step 2 : Base Word Meaning = ...
   Step 3 : New Word Meaning = ...

2. How do they predict the weather? Most of the time, their reports are incorrect.

   Step 1 : Prefix = ...
   Step 2 : Use the context.
   Step 3 : Predict = ...

Jennifer: *Hi, guys! Speaking time! Today, I'll be your colleague, friend, and student! Let's start!*

1. **상황: 회사 회식이 끝난 후 집으로 돌아가는 분위기**

You: That was fun! Now how will you get home?
(참 재미있었어요. 이제 어떻게 댁으로 가실 건가요?)
Colleague: I need to go to the nearby subway station.
(저는 근처 지하철 역으로 가야 돼요.)
You: ....
(제가 태워드릴게요.)
Colleague: Thanks a lot! (고맙습니다!)

2. **상황: 회사에서 친구랑 전화로 수다 떨고 있는데 사장님이 갑자기 나타남**

You: Then we saw a movie. It was great!
(그 다음에 영화 보러 갔는데 정말 재미있었어!)
Friend: What did you see? (뭐 봤는데?)
You: Oh. My boss's here! (사장님이 오셨어!)
....
(나중에 다시 전화할게!)
Friend: Sure. (알겠어)

3. **상황: 교실 벽에 낙서를 한 것으로 의심되는 학생이 있는데 증거가 부족한 상황이므로 일단 학생을 믿어주기로 함**

You: Did you scribble on the wall?
(벽에 낙서했니?)
Student: No. (아니요.)
You: Can I believe you? (믿어도 될까?)
Student: Yes. (네.)
You: OK. ....
((의심은 가지만) 믿어줄게.)

Jennifer: *On this last page, you'll do a final review of today's lesson. I'll read aloud five Korean sentences. Please express them in English, OK? Write sentences and check the example sentences.*

1. **제임스한테 이 책 좀 전해줄래?**

   ....

2. **(친구에게) 아버지는 나를 꼬옥 안아주셨어.**

   ....

3. **(부엌에서 남편이 아내에게) 뭐 좀 도와줄까?**

   ....

4. **김교수님께서 이번 토요일에 오프라인 강의를 하실 예정이다.**

   .... this Saturday.

5. **(어머니가 자녀에게) 네 동생(brother) 좀 그만 괴롭혀!**

   Stop ....

LESSON 7

THE VERB, GET

CONTENTS

—

QUESTION OF THE DAY

Jennifer: *Hello! How are you? Today, we'll have another fun class! Before we get started, as usual, let me ask a question. Of course, I know some of you are married, but just imagine that you are single. OK? So, how would you say the following in English?* 저는 내일 결혼합니다.

....

LISTEN AND UNDERSTAND

Jennifer: *Now please listen to the following and answer my questions.*

Jennifer: Next week's my sister's birthday. I want to **get something for her**. Any ideas?
Mike: What does she like?
Jennifer: She loves handbags.
Mike: Then how about **getting her a nice handbag**?
Jennifer: Well, you know, women's handbags are very expensive in Korea.
Mike: Oh. Well, you have enough time. You can think about it some more.

1. When is my sister's birthday?

....

2. What does she love?

....

3. Am I going to buy a handbag for my sister?

....

A. Word Study : Get

Get = change of state, become (+adjective)

- It's **get**ting hot / warm / cold / chilly.
- It's **get**ting late.
- I **got** hungry / angry / mad / sick / bored / tired.

Get = receive, be given

- I **get** a lot of junk mail every day.
- I want to **get** a pair of boots for Christmas.
- I **got** an A in English.

Get = obtain (through effort, chance etc.)

- Can you believe it? I **got** a four-year scholarship!

To the Public

Excuse me! Can I **get** your attention, please?

Get = buy: get (somebody) something

- I like your jacket! Where did you **get** it?
- Can you **get** (me) a loaf of bread at the bakery?

Get = bring: get (somebody) (something)

- Can you go back and **get** (me) my car keys?

(Husband to Wife)

A: I'll **get** the kids from school.

B: Then, I'll make a delicious dinner!

Get = arrive, reach

- I **got** to Seoul at 7 pm.
- I'll **get** there in a minute.
- Yesterday I **got** home at midnight.

Get = catch an illness

- I think/feel like I'm **get**ting a cold.* I feel chilly.
- I **got** food poisoning last week.

Get = answer the door / phone

(Ding-Dong)

I'll **get** the door!

(Ring-Ring)

Son! Will you **get** the phone?

Get = be punished

- He only **got** 5 years in prison.

* 또는 I think / feel like I'm coming down with a cold.

B. Idioms / Proverbs

Try to guess the meaning of each idiom or proverb before you watch the lecture.

- contact someone by calling or writing (including e-mail) [연락하다]
- find the truth about a situation [원인을 밝혀내다, 진상을 규명하다]
- don't want to continue doing something because you get afraid or nervous [(계획했던 일에 대해) 갑자기 초조해지다, 겁이 나다]
- understand a situation (by yourself or by hearing from someone) [상황을 이해하다, 상황 파악이 되다]
- One does not express things directly, but you understand him/her. [말로 표현되지 않은 것을 알아차리다, 뜻을 알아채다]

Get the message

1. Okay, you don't need to say any more. I **get the message**.

   = ...

Get the picture

2. A: Oh, I see why she got upset!

   B: Now you **get the picture**!

   = ...

Get cold feet

3. I was going to propose to her, but suddenly I **got cold feet**. She might say no!

   = ...

Get to the bottom of something

4. The police must **get to the bottom of this celebrity sex scandal**. Otherwise, this will happen again.

   = ...

Get in touch (with someone)

5. (Friends at the Airport)

   A: Okay. Time to say goodbye.

   B: I'll **get in touch with you** when I have time!

   = ...

LESSON 7

C. Phrasal Verbs: Get (...) up / Get on / off ... *

Try to guess the meaning of each phrasal verb before you watch the lecture.

> (Mom to Child in the Morning)
>
> A: Oh no! Are you still in bed? I can't believe it! **Get up**!
>
> B: I'm so sleepy. Can you **get me up** in 30 minutes again?

1. "Get (someone) up" means: ....

> (Colleagues Waiting for a Bus to Go Home)
>
> A: Which bus are you waiting for?
>
> B: 100.
>
> A: Oh, here it comes - you should **get on that bus**!

2. "Get on the bus/the subway/the train" means: ....

* 또는 get on/off **an airplane** vs. get in/out of **a car (a taxi, a truck, a van)**

(Mom to Daughter on the Phone)

A: I missed my stop!

B: Mom! You always do that! Don't call me once you get on the bus, Okay?

A: All right. I'll **get off the bus** at the next stop.

3. "Get off the bus / the subway / the train" means: ....

D. This is Confusing!

철수: 교수님, I **have** a cold와 I'**m getting** a cold에 의미 차이가 있나요? 그리고 I'**m getting** a cold와 같은 뜻으로 I'**m having** a cold도 가능한가요?

교수님: 좋은 질문입니다. 그럼 잘 들어보세요!

(Friends)

A: You look sick.

B: I **have** a cold.

(= You're already sick because of a cold.)

(Friends)

A: You look sick.

B: I think I'm **getting** a cold. (OK)

(= You don't have a cold yet, but you're about to)

→ I think I'm **having** a cold. (NOT OK)

E. Variety / Register / Nuance: Marry vs. Get married

A: John and Ann are so in love with each other!

B: ***(More Formal)*** I think they'll **marry** soon.

(More Casual/Common) I think they'll **get married** soon.

A: Every time I see John and Ann, they're always arguing with each other.

B: ***(More Formal)*** I spoke with John the other day, and he said they are likely to **divorce** eventually.

(More Casual/Common) I talked to John the other day. He said they are likely to **get divorced**.

F. Word Parts: Prefixes (anti- / sub-)

Anti- / Sub- + Base Word = Against / Under

Anti- + war (N)	=	Anti-war (Adj.)
Sub- + way (N)	=	Subway (N)

- What's this movie about? It's an anti-war movie.
- A child asks, "Why is the subway underground?"

Guess the meaning of each underlined word. Follow the three steps.

1. A lot of criminals are antisocial. They're against society and people.

   Step 1: Antisocial = ... + ...

   Step 2: Base Word Meaning = ...

   Step 3: New Word Meaning = ...

2. Some people call 박태환 "마린보이." Then what does submarine mean?

   Step 1: Submarine = ... + ...

   Step 2: Base Word Meaning = ...

   Step 3: New Word Meaning = ...

LESSON 7

Jennifer: *Today, I'll play your friend in all three dialogs! Are you guys ready?*

1. **상황: 카메라를 사러 백화점에 온 친구들**

You: .... (저기 카메라 좀 봐!)

Friend: Let's go inside and check it out!
(안에 들어가서 한번 살펴보자!)

You: Wait! (잠깐만!) .... (배고프려고 그래.)
Why don't we eat first? (우리 먼저 먹는 게 어때?)

Friend: Sure. (알았어.)

2. **상황: 표를 예매하러 왔는데 줄이 너무 길어서 당황해하는 친구들**

Friend: Look at the long line! (저 줄 좀 봐!)

You: I didn't expect this.
(이렇게 사람들이 많을 줄 예상하지 못했는데.)

Friend: The tickets might be all sold out! (매진될지도 모르겠는데!)

You: Don't worry. (걱정하지 마.)
John's already in line. (존이 이미 줄을 서고 있어.)
Let's ask him to ....
(우리 티켓도 예매해달라고 하자.)

3. **상황: 친구의 데이트가 어땠는지 묻고 있음**

Friend: How was your date? (데이트 어땠어?)

You: ....
(나한테 별 관심이 없더라고.)

Friend: How do you know that? (그걸 어떻게 알아?)

You: She wouldn't give me her number.
(나한테 전화번호를 주려고 하지 않더라고.)
....
(그래서 눈치챘지 뭐.)

Jennifer: *On this last page, you'll do a final review of today's lesson. I'll read aloud five Korean sentences. Please express them in English, OK? Write sentences and check the example sentences.*

1. 남자친구한테서 편지(letter) 받았어.

2. (비서가 손님에게) 뭐 좀 드릴까요? Coffee or tea?

3. 저는 보통 밤 12시에 집에 도착합니다.

4. John에게 연락을 해야 되는데요.

5. (어머니가 아들에게) 가서 아빠 좀 깨워줄래?

LESSON 9

HEALTH & FEELINGS

CONTENTS

QUESTION OF THE DAY

Jennifer: *Hello, everyone! How was your midterm exam? Did you do a good job? Well, the exam is over, and we can't do anything about it. But we can express how we feel about the exam, right? So, that's my question for today. How would you say the following in English?* 시험 결과가 굉장히 걱정스러워요.

READ AND UNDERSTAND

Jennifer: *Now please read the following with me and answer my questions.*

> Today, **I'm very anxious**. Do you know why? My midterm exams start today. Did I tell you that I'm a graduate student? I'm majoring in English education. Actually, this is my first semester, so I'm taking my first exam today. **I'm very nervous and worried**. **Unfortunately, I didn't sleep well last night**, so **I feel very tired**, too. But **I hope I can do a good job today and feel proud**! You know, studying and working at the same time **is not an easy thing**. But I think if I do my best in both areas, I'll have good results.

1. I'm going to graduate this semester. ***True*** ***False***

2. Today I'm very tired because I did not sleep well last night.

   True ***False***

3. I want to do well on my exam today and feel proud.

   True ***False***

A. Theme Study: Health & Feelings

Health = common symptoms / ailments / diseases

A: You look **tired**.

B: Yeah, I'm not feeling **good**.

A: Your face is so **pale**!

B: I think I'm getting **sick**.* I feel very **cold**.

(Doctor to Patient)

A: What can I do for you today?

B: I'm constantly **sneez**ing / **cough**ing / **blow**ing **my nose**! **

- I've lost **my appetite / voice**.
- I have **a headache / a toothache / a stomachache / an earache**.
- I have **a cold / the flu / a cough / a sore throat / a temperature**.
- I have **indigestion / insomnia / asthma / sunburn / heartburn**.
- I have **diarrhea / a hangover**.
- He died because he had **a heart attack**.

Health = injuries

A: I **cut/nicked** my finger while (I was) cooking! / I **cut** myself while shaving.

B: Be careful!

A: Did you **hurt** your ankle / leg?

B: Yeah, I **twisted (=sprained) / broke** it.

Compare My ankle/leg **hurt**s.

A: You **have a bruise** on your knee!

B: Yeah, I fell down the stairs.

* 또는 I feel like I'm getting a cold. (vs. 'a full blown cold')
** 또는 I have a runny nose.

A: I **burned** my finger while (I was) using the stove. / I **burned** myself on the iron.

B: Oops! It looks very **painful**!

Compare I **burn** quite easily.

Feelings = mental

- I'm **pleased**/**glad**/**happy**/**delighted**.
- I'm **excited**/**enthusiastic**/**thrilled**/**hyper**.
- I'm **thankful**/**grateful**.

- I'm **annoyed (= irritated)**/**angry**/**mad**.
- I'm **worried**/**nervous**/**anxious**/**stressed (out)**/**depressed**.
- I'm **afraid**/**frightened**/**scared**.
- I'm **jealous**/**confused**/**ashamed**/**embarrassed**.

Feelings = physical

- I'm/feel **full**/**warm**/**hot**.
- I'm/feel **hungry**/**thirsty**/**shivery**.
- I'm/feel **dizzy**/**nauseous**.*

Feelings = likes/wants/hopes

- I **like**/**love**/**hate** action movies.
- I don't **like** action movies.

- I **want/I'd like** a new pair of shoes on my birthday.
- I **want to/I'd like to** get a new pair of shoes on my birthday.

- I **hope to** get a new pair of shoes for Christmas.
- I **hope** (**that**) I can get a new pair of shoes for Christmas.

* 추가적인 표현으로 throw up, vomit, pass out, faint

B. Idioms / Proverbs

Try to guess the meaning of each idiom or proverb before you watch the lecture.

- feel that you want to do something […을 할 기분이다]
- be happy / be angry or depressed [기분이 좋다 / 언짢다]
- be bored with or annoyed by something / someone
  […에 싫증 나다, 진저리 나다]
- have both positive and negative feelings [기분이 복잡하다, 착잡하다]
- Don't feel sad or depressed. More chances will come.
  [세상이 끝난 것은 아니다, 용기를 내라]

Have mixed feelings (about someone / something)

1. A: You're finally graduating today! Are you happy?
   B: Well, I **have mixed feelings**. I'm worried about a job.

   = ...

Be in a good / bad mood

2. Your dad'**s in a good mood**. If you want a bike, tell him now.

   = ...

Be in the mood (for something / to V)

3. (Husband to Wife)
   A: Let's eat out tonight!
   B: Sounds good! I'**m in the mood for Thai food**!

   = ...

Be sick and tired of something / someone

4. I'm **sick and tired of studying**! I study every week and weekend!

   = ...

It's not the end of the world!

5. (Child to Mother)

   A: I didn't do a good job on the exam.

   B: It's OK. **It's not the end of the world**. You'll do better next time!

   = ...

C. Phrasal Verbs : Cheer (...) up (...) / Calm (...) down (...)

Try to guess the meaning of each phrasal verb before you watch the lecture.

> (Two Friends Talking)
>
> A: Hey, **cheer up**! That wasn't a big mistake.
>
> B: I know, but I just feel stupid.

1. "Cheer (someone) up / Cheer up (someone)" means: ....

   ....

> (Crying Mom to Policeman)
>
> A: I've lost my son!
>
> B: OK, ma'am, but you need to **calm down**, first.

2. "Calm (someone) down / Calm down (someone)" means: ....

   ....

D. This is Confusing!

철수: 교수님, '저는 액션 영화를 싫어합니다'라고 표현하려면 **dis-** 접두사를 이용해서 I **dislike** action movies라고 하면 될까요?

교수님: 좋은 질문입니다. 그럼 잘 들어보세요!

Positive Statement

- I **like** action movies.

Negative Statement

More Common:

I **don't like** action movies.

Less Common:

I **dislike** action movies.

E. Variety / Register / Nuance: Sick vs. Ill

Americans tend to say

A: Where's Jason?

B: He's at home. He's **sick**. (=unwell)

The British tend to say

A: Where's Jason?

B: He's at home. He's **ill**. (=unwell)

F. Word Parts: Suffixes (-able / -ly)

Base Word + -able / -ly = Adjective Marker / Adverb Marker

Fashion (N) + -able	=	Fashionable (Adj.)
Happy (Adj.) + -ly	=	Happily (Adv.)

- This clothing style is becoming fashionable again.
- Once upon a time, a princess was born… They lived happily ever after.

Guess the meaning of each underlined word. Follow the three steps.

1. I have such a comfortable bed. It's old but is still very relaxing when I sleep in it.

   Step 1: Comfortable = ...
   Step 2: Comfortable = ... + ...
   Step 3: Base Word Meaning = ...

2. Normally, it takes 20 minutes to get home, but today, it took an hour! There was a car accident!

   Step 1: Normally = ...
   Step 2: Normally = ... + ...
   Step 3: Base Word Meaning = ...

Jennifer: *It's time again to do some speaking practice! Today in the dialogs, I'll do a pharmacist, your friend, and your mother! Are you excited? Let's get started!*

1. **상황: 속이 쓰리고 소화가 안 돼서 약국을 찾음**

Pharmacist: How may I help you, today? (어떻게 오셨어요?)
You: ....
(속이 쓰리고 소화가 잘 안 돼요.)
Pharmacist: When did it start? (언제 그런 증세가 시작되었나요?)
You: .... (일주일 정도 됐어요.)

2. **상황: 친구와 함께 (스마트폰으로) 이번 주말에 어떤 영화를 볼지 살펴보는 중**

Friend: Which movie do you want to see?
(무슨 영화 보고 싶어?)
You: I don't know what's out there, but
(무슨 영화가 상영되는지는 잘 모르겠지만),
....
(난 로맨틱 코미디 좋아해.)
Friend: (Looking on the screen of her smartphone) OK. Let's see what's showing this weekend.
(이번 주말에 어떤 영화가 상영되고 있는지 한번 보자).
You: ....
(넌 어떤 종류의 영화가 좋아?)

3. **상황: 학교에서 무슨 일이 있었는지 (사춘기의) 아이 표정이 좋지 않음**

Mom: What's the matter, honey? (표정이 왜 그래?)
You: (Silence)
Mom: Something happened in school? (학교에서 무슨 일 있었어?)
You: I'm sorry, mom, but (죄송하지만, 엄마……)
....
(지금 말할 기분이 아니에요.)

Jennifer: *On this last page, you'll do a final review of today's lesson. I'll read aloud five Korean sentences. Please express them in English, OK? Write sentences and check the example sentences.*

1. **(추워서 몸을 떨고 있는 상황) 몸을 떨고 있네! 안으로 들어와서 몸 좀 녹여!**

   You're shivering! ....

2. **(지난 밤에 과음을 한 후) 아직도 숙취가 남아 있네.**

   ....

3. **(엄마가 아픈 아이에게) 아직도 열나는지 보자.**

   Let's see if ....

4. **요즘 스트레스가 너무 심해.**

   ....

5. **어제 요리하다가 손가락이 베였어.**

   While (I was) cooking yesterday, ...

LESSON 10

APPEARANCE & CHARACTER

CONTENTS

QUESTION OF THE DAY

Jennifer: *Hi, students! How're you feeling today? Are you feeling good? Great! In today's lesson, we're going to learn how to describe people's appearance and character. Here's an example. How would you say the following in English?* 그분 참 좋은 사람이에요.

....

LISTEN AND UNDERSTAND

Jennifer: *Now please listen to the following and answer my questions.*

(Mike Looking at Jennifer's Sister's Photo)

Mike: Is this your sister?

Jennifer: Yep, that's right! She's **pretty**, isn't she?

Mike: Yeah. And she looks very **friendly**.

Jennifer: She has a lot of friends and gets along well with new people.

Mike: I see. She also looks quite **tall**. How **tall** is she?

Jennifer: I'm not sure, but maybe almost 170 centimeters?

Mike: Wow. So **taller** than you.

1. Mike has met my sister before. ***True*** ***False***

2. My sister likes to talk to other people. ***True*** ***False***

3. I'm shorter than my sister. ***True*** ***False***

A. Theme Study : Appearance & Character

Appearance = height

- My dad is very **tall**, but my mom is very **short**.

  Compare My dad is very high, but my mom is very low. (X)

A: How **tall** are you?

B: I'm 163 centimeters (tall). As a Korean woman, I think I'm **average height**.

Appearance = weight / build

- My sister is **slim**, but I'm **overweight**. I need to **lose weight**.

A: Look at the baby!

B: He's so **cute**! Look at his **chubby** cheeks!

(New Mother to Nurse)

A: How much does my baby **weigh**?

B: He **weighs** 3.5 kilograms.

- My brother "lives" in a gym. He wants to look **muscular / well-built**.

Appearance = age

- My son is a **teenager / in his teens**.
- My daughter is **in her** (**early / mid- / late**) **30's**.

(Talking about the Third Person)

A: How **old** is she?

B: I think she's **thirty-something / in her 30's**.

I think she's **thirtyish / somewhere around 30**.

- My mom is 50, **middle aged**, yet she has a really young mindset!

Appearance = looks

- Generally, African Americans have **dark skin**. Asians have **light/fair skin**.
- My mom and I have **curly hair**, but my dad has **straight hair**.
- I have (**short/long**) **blonde/brown/black hair**.
- White people (or Caucasians) have various eye colors, but Asians commonly have (**dark**) **brown eyes**.
- My grandfather has **a beard** and **a mustache**.

Character = positive

- Rick is very **nice/kind/friendly**. Everyone likes him.
- My teacher is a **great/wonderful** person. Many students **respect** him.
- Jane is very **thoughtful**. She always thinks about the feelings of other people.

- My mother may be the most **generous** person in the world.
- Mrs. Kim's children are **well-behaved**. They have good manners.
- She's one of the most successful CEOs, yet she's very **humble**.

- Most of the time, I am **honest/frank** with people.
- My youngest child is very **sociable**. He wants to talk to everyone!
- **Optimistic** people are usually happy. They **think positively** about things.
- Most of the students at HYCU are very **hard-working**. They have their own dreams.

Character = negative

- Rick is very nice, but his brother is very **mean** (**to** me).
- Jane is very thoughtful, but her sister is very **selfish**.
- Sometimes, adults get **childish** over little things. They act like children.

- My husband is very **stubborn**. He doesn't listen to anyone.
- He's so **stingy**. He never buys me coffee or anything.
- Wendy is too **arrogant**. She thinks that she is more important than other people.

- These days, some young people are very **rude to** older people.
- Some people are very **cruel to** animals. They are not toys. They are living things!
- **Pessimistic** people are usually **depressed**. They think that bad things will happen.
- If you are **lazy**, you'll never succeed with anything in your life.

B. Idioms / Proverbs

Try to guess the meaning of each idiom or proverb before you watch the lecture.

- an ordinary person [보통의 평범한 남자, 여자]
- manage/fail to control one's anger [화를 참다/화를 내다]
- like/unlike one's usual character [(성격상) …다운/…답지 않은]
- Don't judge people or things based on how they look outside.
  [겉모습만 보고 판단해서는 안 된다]
- People have different thoughts about what is beautiful.
  [아름다움은 보는 이의 생각에 달려 있다, 제 눈에 안경]

In/Out of character

1. As usual, she was acting **in character**. She walked away when the argument started.

   I can't believe he acted that way! He's usually very humble, but today he was **out of character**! So arrogant!

   = ...

Keep / Lose one's temper

2. I try hard to **keep my temper** when my children misbehave.
   I **lost my temper** over nothing again! How can I control my anger?

   = ...

Average Joe (Jane)

3. (Neighbor Describing Neighbor to Police)
   He seemed to be **an average Joe** with a wife and two children. They appeared to be happy, but recently ....

   = ...

Beauty is in the eye of the beholder.

4. A: The baby looked ugly to me, but other people said she was adorable.
   B: Well, **beauty is in the eye of the beholder**.

   = ...

You can't judge a book by its cover.

5. A: Did you know that he's a millionaire? He always takes the subway to work!
   B: Well, **you can't judge a book by its cover**!

   = ...

C. Phrasal Verbs
: (Be) dress(ed) up / Show (...) off / Show off (...)

Try to guess the meaning of each phrasal verb before you watch the lecture.

(Friends Talking)

A: What's the occasion? You**'re** really **dressed up**!*

B: I have a job interview today.

1. "(Be) dress(ed) up" means: ....

(Friends Whispering)

A: Why did she want to see us?

B: She wants to **show off her new boyfriend**!

2. "Show (somebody/something) off/Show off (somebody/something)" means: ....

D. This is Confusing!

철수: 교수님, She's **thirtyish** 라는 표현을 이번 수업에서 배웠는데, 참 독특한 표현 같아요. **-ish** 를 이용한 다른 예들이 또 있을까요?

교수님: 좋은 질문입니다. 그럼 잘 들어보세요!

A: What time do you want to get up tomorrow?

B: **7ish**. (= about 7)

A: What color was it?

B: I can't remember precisely, but it was **yellowish**. (= slightly yellow)

* 또는 You really dressed up. / You've really dressed up.

E. Variety / Register / Nuance: Skinny vs. Slim

Usually Negative Nuance	*More Positive Nuance*
Skinny	Slim / Slender
Fat	Overweight / Large

A: I'm going to lose weight. I want to look **skinny**!
B: What? You want to look **skinny**? Why?

A: I'm going to lose weight. I want to look **slim**!
B: Good luck!

F. Word Parts: Suffixes (-ful / -ous)

Base Word + -ful / -ous = Adjective Marker / Adjective Marker

Beauty (N) + -ful	=	Beautiful (Adj.)
Glamor (N) + -ous	=	Glamorous (Adj.)

- To me, my mother is the most beautiful woman in the world.
- At every awards ceremony, actresses appear so glamorous in their gorgeous dresses.

Guess the meaning of each underlined word. Follow the three steps.

1. As we get older, we slowly lose our memory. We become forgetful.

Step 1: Forgetful = ... + ...
Step 2: Base Word Meaning = ...
Step 3: New Word Meaning = ...

2. This food is so delicious! Can I have more?

Step 1 : Suffix = ... → Part of Speech = ...

Step 2 : Use the context.

Step 3 : Delicious = ...

VOCABULARY USE IN DIALOG

Jennifer: *Welcome back, students! Today, we have very fun dialogs again. In these dialogs, I'll be your friend and neighbor! Let's begin!*

1. **상황: 가까이 지내는 어린 친구가 있는데 인생의 선배로서 조언을 하려고 함**

You: ....
(조언 하나 해도 될까?)

Friend: Uh... Yeah! Please. (어⋯⋯ 네! 해 주세요.)

You: Don't ....
(다른 사람들에게 너무 네 속을 보이는 건 그리 좋지 않아.)

Friend: Oh, I know what you mean.
(무슨 말인지 알겠어요.)
Yeah, I sometimes go too far. I'll be careful!
(맞아요. 제가 가끔은 너무 그렇죠. 조심할게요!)

2. **상황: 초등학교 동창생을 만나서 옛날 얘기를 하다가 뒤늦은 고백을 들음!**

You: .... at the time.
(너, 그때 나한테 정말 못되게 굴었어.)

Old Friend: Well, actually... I had a crush on you.
(음, 사실은⋯⋯ 너 좋아했었어.)

You: Really? You should've just told me.
(정말? 그럼 그렇다고 얘기를 하지.)

Old Friend: Well, when people are young, they often express their feelings that way. (어릴 때는 그렇게 표현하잖아.)

3. **상황: 내 아이들이 예의 바르다고 이웃에게서 칭찬을 듣는데 그리 기쁘지 않음**

Neighbor : Your children are so well-behaved.
(아이들이 굉장히 예의가 바르네요.)

You : ....
(글쎄, 겉만 보고는 알 수가 없는 것이랍니다.)

Neighbor : What do you mean? (무슨 말이에요?)

You : ....
(녀석들이 얼마나 고집이 센데요!)

FINAL REVIEW

Jennifer: *On this last page, you'll do a final review of today's lesson. I'll read aloud five Korean sentences. Please express them in English, OK? Write sentences and check the example sentences.*

1. **그 사람은 참 겸손해요.**

....

2. **그 사람은 참 사교성이 좋아요.**

....

3. **유치하게 굴지 마, 좀!**

....

4. **게으른 사람은 절대(never) 인생에서 성공할 수가 없답니다.**

....

5. **무슨 일이야? 멋지게 입었네!**

What's the occasion? ....

LESSON 11

WORK & OFFICE PROBLEMS

CONTENTS

QUESTION OF THE DAY

Jennifer: *Hello, students! Hope you're all doing well! Both at work and at school! Today's topic is work! When we work, we get paid. But if possible, we want to have more money, right? So, how would you say the following in English?* 월급 인상 좀 받을 수 있을까요?

....

READ AND UNDERSTAND

Jennifer: *Now please read the following with me and answer my questions.*

> You know that I'm a graduate student, and I'm **work**ing **full-time** at HYCU. How's that possible? I go to an online graduate school, so I can study and **work** at the same time. But as you know, this isn't easy. Since I **have a full-time job**, I **work 9 to 6**. But I'm glad that I **have a job** because I can pay my tuition. These days, it's so difficult to **find a job**, you know. Also, I **like my job**! As I mentioned before, I like teaching. So, I can't complain. And next year, I might **get a raise**! So I'll **earn more money**. If I get more money, I'll go back to the U.S. for a vacation!

1. I'm a full-time student and work part-time. ***True*** ***False***
2. I'm studying at an offline graduate school. ***True*** ***False***
3. Next year I might earn more money. ***True*** ***False***

A. Theme Study : Work & Office Problems

Work = looking for a Job

(Interviewer to Interviewee)

A: **What's your current job?**

B: I'm **an office worker**.

A: Why do you want to **get/find a** new **job**?

(Interviewer to Interviewee)

A: Where do you work now?

B: I **work at** McDonald's.

A: Is that **a full-time job**?

B: No, I **work part-time**, from 7 to 10 pm.

(Interviewer to Interviewee)

A: This job **involves** (a lot of) traveling. Is that OK?

B: Yes, no problem.

(Interviewer to Interviewee)

A: **What kind of work** do you usually **do** as a secretary?

B: I **make appointments**, **prepare meetings**, **send emails**, and **receive calls**.

(Interviewee to Interviewer)

A: I'm **a free-lancer writer**.

B: So, you usually **work at home**?

Work = employed

(Colleagues)

A: Hey, let's go. **It's lunch break**!

B: Actually, I brought my lunch. I'**m on a diet**. But I can go with you!

(Wife to Husband on the Phone)

A: Hello?

B: Guess what! I **got promoted/a promotion**!

(Boss to Employee)

A: What is it?

B: Um... **Would you** consider **giving me a raise**?

Compare Can I get a raise? (Not polite enough)

(Colleagues)

A: Where's John?

B: He**'s off** today. He's **taking a sick day**.

(Colleagues Talking About Union Strike)

A: They **went on strike** yesterday.

B: Are you going to **join the strike**?

(Colleagues)

A: If you **retire**, what are you going to do?

B: I'll **do some volunteer work**. I might teach English to **low-income** students.

Work = unemployed

(Husband to Wife)

A: I **quit** my job. I can't **stand** my boss!

B: Not again!

(Roommates)

A: Why do you read the job ad section all day long?

B: Well, I **got fired/laid off**. So, I need to **find a new job**.

Office Problems = photocopiers / printers / paper

A: What's the matter?

B: I don't have time, but the photocopier **is not working** / **has broken down** again!

A: What's the matter?

B: The printer **is jammed**, and I**'ve run out of paper**!

(coffee maker) **out of order** (copier) **malfunction**

(computer) **crash** (monitor) **freeze** (system) **down**

B. Idioms / Proverbs

Try to guess the meaning of each idiom or proverb before you watch the lecture.

- (praise) do something well [잘했어!]
- It is OK with me. […에게 적절하다, 좋다, 괜찮다]
- Time resolves everything. [시간이 기적을 베푼다, 시간이 모든 것을 해결해준다]
- You work too much and do not take time to relax.
  [일/공부하기만 하고 쉬지/놀지 않는 것, 너무 일/공부만 하는 것]
- If several people help one person with a large task, they can finish it easily and quickly. [일손이 많으면 일이 쉬워진다, 백지장도 맞들면 낫다]

Good/nice job!

1. (Boss to Employee)

   A: Your presentation was very good. **Good** / **nice job**!

   B: Thanks!

   = ...

All work and no play

2. Your life is **all work and no play**! You should find a hobby!

= ....

(It) works for me.

3. (Gym Trainer to Two Trainees)

A: Is Saturday good for our second work out?

B: **Works for me**!

C: **Works for me**, too!

= ....

Many hands make light work.*

4. (Mother to Children)

A: I have to clean the bathroom, do the dishes, do the laundry...

B: Don't worry, mom! We'll help you. **Many hands make light work**!

= ....

Time works wonders.**

5. I never thought that I could forgive him. But now after 10 years, I don't hate him any longer. It's all in the past. I guess **time works wonders**.

= ....

* 또는 The more, the merrier.
** 또는 Time heals all wounds.

C. Phrasal Verbs : Work out / Work on...

Try to guess the meaning of each phrasal verb before you watch the lecture.

(Friends Talking)

A : You're in good shape. Do you exercise much?

B : Yeah, I **work out** three times a week.

1. "Work out" means : ....

(Friends Talking)

A : What are you studying these days?

B : I'm **work**ing **on** my listening skills. So I listen to English radio shows a lot.

2. "Work on something" means : ....

D. This is Confusing!

철수: 교수님, 알코올중독자를 표현할 때 alco**holic** 이라고 하잖아요. 그럼 일 중독자는 work**aholic** 인가요?

교수님: 좋은 질문입니다. 그럼 잘 들어보세요!

(Wife to Husband)

A: If you keep on drinking, you're going to become **an alcoholic**!

B: Sorry, honey. I had to go for a drink.

A: Yeah, every time you have a reason!

(Colleagues Whispering)

A: Doesn't he have a life? He practically lives in the office!

B: I know! I think he's **a workaholic**. He works even on the weekends!

E. Variety / Register / Nuance
: (Pay) Raise vs. (Pay) Rise

Americans tend to say

(Boss to Employee)

A: What is it?

B: Um… Would you consider giving me **a** (**pay**) **raise**?

(Boss to Secretary)

A: Where's my **schedule**? [skedʒu:l]

B: Here it is.

The British tend to say

(Boss to Employee)

A: What is it?

B: Um…Would you consider giving me **a** (**pay**) **rise**?

(Boss to Secretary)

A: Where's my **schedule**? [ʃedju:l]

B: Here it is.

F. Word Parts: Suffixes (-er / -or)

Base Word + -er / -or = Person / Thing That Does Something

Write (V) + -er	=	Writer (N)
Act (V) + -or	=	Actor (N)

- I love writing and movies, so a screen(play) writer would be a good job for me.
- When I was young, I was very shy. But now I'm an actor, a famous movie star!

Guess the meaning of each underlined word. Follow the three steps.

1. What makes a consumer spend money in a store?

   Step 1 : Consumer = ...

   Step 2 : Consumer = ... + ...

   Step 3 : Base Word Meaning = ...

2. My father spends most of his time on the ocean. He works on a ship. He is a sailor.

   Step 1 : Sailor = ...

   Step 2 : Sailor = ... + ...

   Step 3 : Base Word Meaning = ...

Jennifer: *Well, students, are you having fun? Let's see if you can express yourself in a dialog. Here we go!*

1. **상황: 드라마 오디션을 보러 온 현직 뉴스앵커를 인터뷰 하는 중**

You: .... , aren't you?
(현직 뉴스 앵커이시잖아요.)
Interviewee: Yes. (네.)
You: Hmm... ....
(그런데 그만두시려고요?)
Interviewee: I've always wanted to be an actor.
(항상 배우가 되고 싶었거든요.)

2. **상황: 옛 시절의 연인을 만나게 되어 조심스럽게 근황에 대해 이야기를 나눔**

Ex-boy/girlfriend: Where do you work?
(어디서 일해?)
You: ....
(작은 회사에서 일해.)
Ex-boy/girlfriend: Oh, great! Are you... married?
(결혼은…… 했어?)
You: Yeah. ....
(애가 두 명이야.)

3. **상황: 어머니가 아들의 출근 시간을 착각해 자고 있는 아들을 깨우는 중**

Mother: Aren't you going to work?
(일하러 가야지.)
You: ....
(이번 주는 야간 근무야.)
Mother: Oh, right! Sorry, honey. Go back to sleep.
(아, 맞아.미안하다, 얘야. 어서 다시 자렴.)
You: ....
([엄마가 미안하다고 하니] 괜찮아, 엄마.)

Jennifer: *On this last page, you'll do a final review of today's lesson. I'll read aloud five Korean sentences. Please express them in English, OK? Write sentences and check the example sentences.*

1 **저는 삼성에 다니고 있어요.**

....

2. **이 직업은 말을 많이 해야 합니다.**

....

3. **(바로 옆 복사기를 바라보며) 복사기가 또 말을 안 듣네요!**

....

4. **걱정 마. 시간이 해결해줄 거야.**

....

5. **저는 매일 운동을 합니다.**

....

LESSON 12

TIME & PLACE

CONTENTS

QUESTION OF THE DAY

Jennifer: *Welcome to Lesson 12! In this lesson, we're going to learn how to describe some basics about time and place! So, the question of the day is* 지금 몇 시예요? *How would you say this in English?*

....

LISTEN AND UNDERSTAND

Jennifer: *Now please listen to the following and answer my questions.*

Jennifer: Oh, wait a minute. **What date is it today**?
Mike: You don't know? It's **the 23rd**!
Jennifer: I almost forgot my dad's birthday! It's **the day after tomorrow**.
Mike: I see. By the way, are things okay with you these days?
Jennifer: Oh... I know what you mean. I've... Oh, no! I left my smartphone **in the restroom**!
Mike: Oh, Jennifer...
Jennifer: Wait a second! Where's my wallet? Did I leave it **in the subway**?

1. Does Mike know today's date?

....

2. When is my dad's birthday?

....

3. Where's my smartphone?

....

A. Theme Study : Time & Place

Time = seconds / minutes / hours

- There are 60 **seconds in a minute**.
- There are 60 **minutes in an hour**.
- There are 24 **hours in a day**.

Time = days / dates

Days

Sunday	Monday	Tuesday	Wednesday
Thursday	Friday	Saturday	

Dates

First (1st)	Sixth (6th)	Eleventh (11th)
Second (2nd)	Seventh (7th)	Twelfth (12th)
Third (3rd)	Eighth (8th)	Thirteenth (13th)
Fourth (4th)	Ninth (9th)	Fourteenth (14th)
Fifth (5th)	Tenth (10th)	

A: **What day is** (**it**) **today**?
B: (**Today's / It's**) **Monday**.

A: **When is** our essay **due**?
B: (It was due) **the day before yesterday**!

A: **The day after tomorrow** is already Saturday!
B: I know! **Time goes by really fast**!

A: When do you want to see the movie?
B: (I want to see it) **Friday night**.

A: What're you going to do **over the weekend**?
B: I'm going to watch my lessons/classes.

A: **What date is (it) today**?

B: (**Today's / It's**) **the 5th / the 13th**.

Time = months / year

Months

January	May	September
February	June	October
March	July	November
April	August	December

A: My birthday is **in December**. How about you?

B: Mine is **in August**.

A: **What month is your birthday**?

B: It's **next month**.

- There are **twelve months in a year**.

Time = seasons

Seasons

Spring Summer Fall / Autumn Winter

A: **What / Which season** do you like the most?

B: I like **spring / summer / fall / winter** the most.

A: When does the first semester start at a Korean university?

B: The first semester starts **in spring**.

Time = o'clock / after / before / around / at / in

A: **What time is it?** *Compare* Which time is it? (X)

B: It's 9 **o'clock**/It's 9 **on the nose**. (= It's **exactly** 9.)

Compare It's 9:20 o'clock. (X)

- It's 20 **after**/**before**/**to**/**till** 9. (= It's 9:20/It's 8: 40.)
- It's **around**/**about** 9 pm.

A: Excuse me. What time does the next train come?

B: It comes **at** 2/**in** 20 minutes.

Place = on / under / above / behind

A: Where's the cat?

B: She's/He's **on**/**under the dining room table**.

A: Where's the annoying fly?

B: It's **above the picture on the wall**.

A: Where are you?

B: I'm standing right **behind you**!

Place = in / at / next to

A: Where's the cat?

B: She's/He's **in my room**/**in the kitchen**/**in the apartment**/**in the house**.

A: Should I meet you somewhere **inside the mall**?

B: No, let's meet **at the** (**east**) **entrance** to the mall.

A: Should I meet you somewhere **inside the mall**?

B: No, I'll be standing outside **next to the bus stop at the east entrance**.

B. Idioms / Proverbs

Try to guess the meaning of each idiom or proverb before you watch the lecture.

- Time is finished. [시간이 다 됐다]
- I haven't seen you in a long time. [오랜만이다]
- Time passes very quickly! [시간이 쏜살같다, 세월이 유수와 같다]
- Time is as important as money, so don't waste it.
  [시간은 돈이다, 허송세월하지 마라]
- speak with someone at an inconvenient time for him/her
  [안 좋은 시간에, 곤란한 시간에 연락하다]

Time flies!

1. (From Wife to Husband)
   Our son is already entering middle school! **Time flies**!

   = ...

Long time no see!

2. I can't remember when I saw you last! **Long time no see**!

   = ...

Catch someone at a bad time

3. (Calling Someone)
   A: Hello … (Sleepy)
   B: Oh, I'm sorry. Did I **catch you at a bad time**?

   = ...

Time's up.

4. **Time's up**! You have to turn in your test sheets now!

   = ...

Time is money.

5. Why are you wasting your time? **Time is money**, you know!

   = ...

C. Phrasal Verbs : Hang out / Get together

Try to guess the meaning of each phrasal verb before you watch the lecture.

TIME & PLACE

(Friends Talking on the Phone)
A : What are you guys doing?
B : We're just **hanging out**. We're watching a DVD together.

1. "Hang out" means : ....

(Friends Talking)
A : Our exams are finally over! Why don't we **get together** next Sunday?
B : Works for me!

2. "Get together" means : ....

D. This is Confusing!

철수: 교수님, Do you have **time**? 과 Do you have **the time**? 은 다른 의미인가요?

교수님: 좋은 질문입니다. 그럼 잘 들어보세요!

A: What time is it?

B: It's 9:20.

A: Do you **have time**? (= Can I talk to you? Can I do something with you?)

B: Uh, yeah. What is it?

A: Do you **have the time**? (= What time is it?)

B: It's 9:20.

E. Variety / Register / Nuance: After vs. Past

Americans tend to say

A: What time is it now?

B: It's a quarter **after** 5. (= It's 5:15.)

A: What date is it today?

B: It's **June 1st, 2013**. (= month / date / year)

The British tend to say

A: What time is it now?

B: It's a quarter **past** 5. (= It's 5:15.)

A: What date is it today?

B: It's **1st June, 2013**. (= date / month / year)

F. Word Parts : Suffixes (-ive / -y)

Base Word + -ive / -y = Adjective Marker / Adjective Marker

Act (V) + -ive	=	Active (Adj.)
Dirt (N) + -y	=	Dirty (Adj.)

- Although my mother is almost 70 years old, she's still very active.
- (Mother to Child) Your hands are so dirty again! What did you do this time?

Guess the meaning of each underlined word. Follow the three steps.

1. Our last meeting wasn't productive at all. We didn't make any progress.

   Step 1 : Productive = ...

   Step 2 : Productive = ... + ...

   Step 3 : Base Word Meaning = ...

2. This old house is quite dusty. Nobody has lived here in a long time!

   Step 1 : Dusty = ...

   Step 2 : Dusty = ... + ...

   Step 3 : Base Word Meaning = ...

Jennifer: *Welcome back, students! Before we start this page, let me ask you a question. What time is it now? Please check the time and tell me what time it is. .. Okay. Thanks for trying! Keep speaking English, okay? Now let's start practicing our mini fun conversations!*

1. **상황: 한양사이버대학교 오프라인 특강 참석을 위해 전화로 만날 약속을 하는 중**

Friend: Where should we meet? (어디서 만나는 게 좋을까?)
You: ....
(1층 커피숍에서 만나자.)
Friend: Is the coffee shop in Cyber Building 1 or 2? I'm confused.
(커피숍이 사이버대 1관에 있어? 아니면 2관에 있어? 헷갈리네.)
You: .... (2관에 있어.)

2. **상황: 한양사이버대학교 오프라인 모임에서 스마트폰으로 무언가를 보는 학우를 봄**

You: .... (지금 뭐하세요?)
Classmate: I'm checking our quiz deadline. (우리 퀴즈 마감일 알아보려고요.)
You: ....
(내일 모레 밤 11시 59분까지인데요.)
Classmate: Oh I see. Thanks for letting me know!
(그렇군요. 알려줘서 고마워요!)

3. **상황: 시간 참 빨리 간다면서 친구와 이야기 나누는 중**

Friend: It's already the end of May! (벌써 5월 말이야!)
You: I know! (그러게 말이야!)
.... (시간 참 빨리 가네!)
Friend: So, finals are coming up again! (그럼 조금 있으면 다시 기말이야.)
You: .... (중간고사 때 못 해서),
so I have to study harder this time!
(이번에는 더 열심히 공부해야 돼!)

Jennifer: *On this last page, you'll do a final review of today's lesson. I'll read aloud five Korean sentences. Please express them in English, OK? Write sentences and check the example sentences.*

1. **오늘이 며칠이에요?**

   ....

2. **오늘은 10월 20일입니다.**

   ....

3. **저는 겨울에 태어났습니다(born).**

   ....

4. **다음 버스는 10분 뒤에 올 것 같아요.**

   I think ....

5. **(숨바꼭질 하면서 엄마가 아이에게) 어디 있을까? 커튼(curtains) 뒤에 숨었나?**

   ....

LESSON 13

WEATHER & NATURAL DISASTERS

CONTENTS

—

QUESTION OF THE DAY

Jennifer: *Hello, students! How are you today? We're getting closer to the end of the semester. I hope you'll keep on focusing on your studies till the semester ends! OK. Today's question is, how would you say* 방금 소나기가 내리기 시작했어 *in English?*

READ AND UNDERSTAND

Jennifer: *Now please read the following with me and answer my questions.*

> Today, I'm going to talk about **the weather! What kind of weather** do you like? Everybody has their **favorite type of weather**. Like most people, I like **bright and sunny weather**. I feel fresh when **the sky** is **clear and blue**. However, I also like **rainy days**. Oh, don't get me wrong! I don't like to be **in the rain**, but I like to hear **the sound of the rain**. I mean, I like **the sound of the rain drops** when they touch the ground, especially when **it rains hard**. For some reason, when I hear these sounds, I feel like my stress goes away. How about you?

1. I like rainy weather because I like to be in the rain.

   True ***False***

2. I also like sunny days because the sky is clear and blue.

   True ***False***

3. The sound of hard-falling rain drops makes my stress go away.

   True ***False***

A. Theme Study : Weather & Natural Disasters

Weather = mild / breeze / humid / dry / drought

(Two Strangers Waiting for a Bus)

A: It's **nice weather**.

Compare It's a nice weather. (X)

B: Yeah, it's really **beautiful**.

- I love **this kind of weather** when **it's mild** and **warm**. It makes me want to take a nap.
- Imagine **a cool breeze** on **a hot summer day**.

(Child Just Woken Up & Asking Mother)

A: **How's the weather going to be today**?

B: Don't worry, honey. **It's bright and sunny**! You can go on your picnic!

- I was born in December. Maybe because of that, I prefer **hot weather** to cold.

(Colleagues)

A: **It's** (**boiling**) **hot** today, isn't it?*

B: Yeah. And **it's** extremely **humid**/**muggy** as well.

- I did my graduate studies in Illinois in the U.S., and I remember **it was very dry** every summer.

- **When is it** ever **going to rain**? All the crops are dying from this **drought**!

* 또는 Today's a scorcher.

Weather = chill(y) / wind(y) / cold / freezing

- I guess we finally **have fall weather**; it's quite **chilly** today.

(Sisters)

A: There's **a lot of wind** today.

B: I hate **windy** days. They ruin my hair.

(Child to Dad)

A: **Is it cold** outside?

B: It's not just cold. **It's freezing** (**cold**)! Be sure to wear a thick coat and a scarf.

Weather = cloud(y) / rain(y) / pour / sprinkle / rain shower

(Child to Mother)

A: Ooh, look at the sky! **It's very cloudy**!

B: **It might rain** / **pour** soon. Don't forget to bring an umbrella with you, okay?

(Friends)

A: Ever since I saw "Sleepless in Seattle," I have fantasized about living there.

B: Well, I hope you like **wet weather**. I hear **it rains** there almost every other day.

(Husband to Wife)

A: **What does the weather forecast say** for today?

B: It says **it's going to be rainy** all afternoon.

(Child to Mother)

A: **It's only sprinkling**. I want to go outside and play.

B: No, you could catch a cold. We'll go outside if it stops, okay?

(Friends)

A: Oh, look out the window! **It looks like a rain shower just started**!

B: Really? **The sky was crystal clear** just a minute ago!

Weather = snow(y) / fog(gy) / lightning

(Wife to Husband)

A: Ooh, look outside! **It's snowing / snowy**!

B: And **it's foggy**, too. Be careful when you drive to work.

- When **the sky gets dark** with clouds, and we **get thunder and lightning**, it makes me really scared.

(Friends from Different Countries)

A: **Is Seoul very cold** in the winter?

B: Yeah. When it's very cold, it can **go down to -20 Celsius**! (= **-4 Fahrenheit**)

Natural Disasters = earthquake / floods / hurricane / tsunami / drown / forest fire

- Japan is notorious for **having a lot of earthquakes**.

(Young Friends)

A: Is your school closed, too?

B: Yeah. The news says that **this hurricane is a really strong one**.

(Friends)

A: Do you remember the last **tsunami** in Japan?

B: Of course. It was so sad that so many people **drowned in the flooding**.

- In the summer, especially **during the dry season, a lot of forest fires break out**.

B. Idioms / Proverbs

Try to guess the meaning of each idiom or proverb before you watch the lecture.

- It's raining very heavily. [비가 억수같이 내린다]
- feel a little sick [몸이 편치 않다, 몸이 좀 안 좋다]
- suspected of having done something wrong
  […이 의심을 받다, 의심스럽다]
- Although one is having difficulties now, s/he will be successful in the end.
  [고생 끝에 낙이 온다]
- someone who is a friend only when you are happy or successful
  [형편이 좋을 때만 친구, 믿을 수 없는 벗]

Be under the weather

1. A: Are you OK? You look pale.
   B: **I'm kind of under the weather**. I didn't sleep well last night.

   = ...

A fair-weather friend*

2. Don't trust people who gather around you only when things are going well with you. Most of them will just be **fair-weather friends**.

   = ...

* 또는 간단히 Not a real friend / Not a true friend

Be under a cloud (of suspicion)

3. Somebody on this bus stole the old lady's wallet. Now **everyone** on the bus **is under a cloud of suspicion**. The police will soon arrive and investigate all the passengers.

   = ...

It's raining cats and dogs.*

4. A: You had an umbrella. Why are you so wet?
   B: **It was raining cats and dogs!**

   = ...

There's (a) light at the end of the tunnel.

5. A: I have too much work and studying to do. It's so difficult to work and go to school at the same time!
   B: Well, **there's light at the end of the tunnel**. This is your last semester, so hang in there and you'll be breathing a sigh of relief in no time.

   = ...

* 또는 It's raining hard/It's pouring outside도 가능한데 좀 더 재미있게 표현하려면 It's raining cats and dogs도 가능

C. Phrasal Verbs : Warm up / Clear up

Try to guess the meaning of each phrasal verb before you watch the lecture.

(Friends at Gym)

A : Hey, why don't we run first?

B : Did you warm up yet? It's important **to warm up** before you work out!

1. "Warm up" means : ....

(Friends Talking)

A : I'm sick and tired of all the rain this week!

B : Relax! The weather forecast says it'll **clear up** tomorrow.

2. "Clear up" means : ....

D. This is Confusing!

철수 : 교수님, 모르는 외국인에게 영어로 말을 걸고 싶을 때 우리나라에서처럼 날씨 얘기로 시작하면 자연스러울까요?

교수님 : 좋은 질문입니다. 그럼 잘 들어보세요!

(Two Strangers Waiting for a Bus)

A: **Nice weather we're having, huh**? (= It's nice weather.)

B: Yeah, it's really beautiful, isn't it?

A: **I guess this is good weather for plants, huh**?

B: **Yeah, it's gotta be good for something**!
(= It's unpleasantly raining, but it must be good for someone/something else.)

E. Variety / Register / Nuance
: Nice weather, we're having, huh?

(Two Strangers Waiting for a Bus on a Sunny Day)

A: **Nice weather we're having, huh? (= It's nice weather.)**

B: Yeah, it's really beautiful, isn't it? (= Yeah, it's really beautiful.)

(Two Strangers Waiting for a Bus on a Cold and Cloudy Day)

A: **Nice weather we're having, huh?* (= It's awful weather.)**

B: Yeah, very nice. (= Yeah, the weather sucks.)

F. Word Parts: Suffixes (-ment / -tion)

Base Word + -ment / -tion = Noun Marker / Noun Marker

Develop (V) + -ment	=	Development (N)
Compete (V) + -tion	=	Competition (N)

- Continuing development in technology has led us to be less creative.
- Is competition in sports good or bad for young children?

Guess the meaning of each underlined word. Follow the three steps.

1. The new president promised a higher employment rate to the citizens.

   Step 1: Employment = ... + ...

   Step 2: Base Word Meaning = ...

   Step 3: New Word Meaning = ...

* sarcasm

2. Some people are dying from starvation. In fact, due to severe drought in certain regions, they don't even have drinkable water.

Step 1 : Starvation = ...

Step 2 : Starvation = ... + ...

Step 3 : Base Word Meaning = ...

VOCABULARY USE IN DIALOG

Jennifer : *Okay. It's time for us to use today's words and expressions in dialogs! Do you remember all the words and expressions from the previous pages? If you're ready, let's go!*

1. **상황 : 인터넷으로 날씨 예보를 체크하다가 내일 날씨에 대해 친구와 이야기함**

Friend : Wow, it looks like summer kicks off tomorrow.
(내일이면 본격적인 여름날씨네!)

You : .... (정말? 내일 덥대?)

Friend : The high's going to be 25. (최고기온이 25도래.)

You : Then, it's time ....
(그럼 슬슬 다이어트 시작해야 되겠는걸!)

2. **상황 : 내일 등산 계획이 있는 친구가 내일 날씨를 물어봄**

Friend : Do you know how the weather's going to be tomorrow?
(내일 날씨 어떨지 알아?)

You : ....
(잘 모르겠는데 스마트폰으로 확인해보면 되지!)

Friend : I hope it's going to be nice. No rain, please.
(날씨가 좋아야 하는데. 제발 비만은 내리지 않기를!)

You : ....
(걱정 안 해도 되겠네 – 비 안 온대.)
.... (그냥 조금 흐릴 거래.)

3. **상황: 어느 날씨 좋은 날 버스를 기다리는 한 외국인 관광객에게 말을 걸어봄**

You: ....
(오늘 날씨 참 좋네요.)

Foreigner: Yeah, it's very nice. (네, 정말 좋네요.)

You: ....
(어느 나라에서 오셨나요?)

Foreigner: I'm from Canada. (캐나다에서 왔어요.)

FINAL REVIEW

Jennifer: *On this last page, you'll do a final review of today's lesson. I'll read aloud five Korean sentences. Please express them in English, OK? Write sentences and check the example sentences.*

1. **오늘 전국적으로(nationwide) 날씨가 굉장히 흐릴(overcast) 거래.**

According to the weather report, ...

.... nationwide.

2. **난 후텁지근한 날씨가 정말 싫어.**

....

3. **비가 억수같이 쏟아지고 있어요!**

....

4. **고생 끝에 낙이 오니까 조금만 참자(patient)!**

....

5. **운동하기 전에 준비운동을 하는 것은 굉장히 중요해!**

....

LESSON 14

LEISURE & VACATIONS

CONTENTS

QUESTION OF THE DAY

Jennifer: *Finally… today is the last day of this course. How has your semester been? Prof. Park and I have enjoyed teaching you. And we hope that you have also enjoyed learning English words and expressions with us. Although we're finishing the course, you'll have to keep learning more English and practice it in everyday situations, OK? The last question for this course is* 어떤 장르의 영화를 가장 좋아하나요? *How would you say this in English?*

....

LISTEN AND UNDERSTAND

Jennifer: *Now please listen to the following and answer my questions.*

(Jennifer in Mike's Apartment)

Jennifer: Wow, look at your **golf clubs**. I didn't know you can **play golf**!

Mike: Oh. You know, back in the States, it's not that expensive to **go golfing**, so I learned a little.

Jennifer: Sounds like fun! Which reminds me, I'm going to **see a baseball game** this weekend.

Mike: Oh yeah? Who are you **rooting for**?

Jennifer: I'm **a big fan of** the Samsung Lions.

Mike: They **beat** the Kia Tigers **11-10** last Saturday, didn't they?

Jennifer: Oh yeah! That was so cool!

1. Mike learned how to play golf in Korea. ***True*** ***False***

2. This weekend I'm going to go and see a basketball game.

True ***False***

3. I root for the Kia Tigers. ***True*** ***False***

A. Theme Study : Leisure & Vacations

Leisure = exercise / sports

A: **Do you exercise much**?

B: Yes. I often **go hiking** with my friends.

Other Exercise go golfing / jogging / swimming / bowling / biking

A: **How do you spend your free time**?

/ **What do you do during your free time**?

B: I love **exercising**, so I **go to a fitness club** near my home.

A: **Do you play any sports**?

B: I **play golf** / **soccer**.

Other Sports play (table) tennis / basketball / baseball / volleyball / badminton

A: Today I'm going to **see a baseball game between** the Samsung Lions **and** the Kia Tigers.

B: So which team are you **supporting** / **rooting for**?

/ So which team **are** you **a fan of**?

(Mother to Mother)

A: My child is so **competitive** when it comes to sports.

B: Well, young boys usually **take sports seriously**. Don't worry too much.

A: I hope he can play **just for fun** sometimes; then he wouldn't be so stressed when he **loses**.

Leisure = scores / records

(Friends Talking About Soccer Match)

A: So what's the score? Please tell me Korea **beat** Japan **3-0**! (= **three to zero**)

B: Actually, that's right. Japan **lost to** Korea 0-3! *

Compare Japan lost to Korea 3-0! (X)

* '동점'은 The game was tied.

(Friends Talking About Badminton Match)

A: We **lost the match**.

B: **By how much?**

A: You won't believe it! We **lost by 10 points**!

(Friends Talking About Table Tennis)

A: **Who's leading*** and **by how much?**

B: China **is leading** Korea, set score **2-1**. (= **two to one**)

(Friends Talking About Sprinter)

A: I can't believe it! He **broke the world record** again!

B: So, he **set a new record** in just about 3 months, huh?

Leisure = movies / theater

A: **What's your favorite movie genre**?

B: I used to love **romantic comedies**, but recently **I've been into disaster movies**.

Other Types

war movie / romance / thriller / action movie / horror movie / comedy

A: I hate (it) when foreign movies **are dubbed** on TV.

B: But I don't like to **read subtitles**, either. I wish I could speak that language!

A: Let's **arrive at the theater 30 minutes early / before (the movie starts) / in advance**.

B: Good idea, but the tickets may already **be sold out**! Let's **get the tickets** online.

Vacations = reservations / order

(Phone Reservation for a Hotel)

A: **Do you have any rooms available**?

B: Sorry, **we're fully booked** at this time.

* 또는 Who's winning?

A: **The total will be / come to** 300 dollars.

B: By the way, **is** breakfast **included** (in the price)?

(Phone Reservation for a Restaurant)

A: **I'd like to book a table / make a reservation for** five people at 7pm tonight - **nonsmoking**, please.

B: Sorry, **our nonsmoking section is fully booked**. How about a table **in the smoking section**?

(Waiter to Customer in a Restaurant)

A: **Are you ready to order**? / Can I **take your order**?

B: Yes, I'**d like** a vegetable and cheese omelet and a glass of orange juice.

A: Would you like to **pay by cash or credit card**?

B: **I'll pay by credit card**. **Here it is**.

(Waiter to Customer at McDonald's)

A: Hello.

B: Hi. I'**ll have** a Big Mac meal. Number 5.

A: (Is this) **for here or to go?**

B: **For here**, **please**.

B. Idioms / Proverbs

Try to guess the meaning of each idiom or proverb before you watch the lecture.

- time off from work [휴가 중이다]
- at a convenient time […에게 편한 때에, …이 시간이 있을 때]
- No problem! / It was easy! / You're welcome!
  [뭘 그런 걸 갖고 그래, 별것 아니야]
- You blame someone for doing something, but you have the wrong person. [잘못 짚다, 엉뚱한 사람을 비난하다]
- The busiest men find the most time for leisure.
  [바쁘게 일하는 사람이 여가 즐길 시간도 있다, 빈둥거리는 사람은 여가 즐길 시간도 없게 된다]

At one's leisure

1. A: When is the most convenient time for me to call you?
   B: You can call **at your leisure**.

   = ...

The busiest men have the most leisure. (Idle people have the least leisure.)*

2. A: John works really hard, yet still finds time for his family and his hobbies!
   B: **The busiest men have the most leisure**!

   = ...

Bark up the wrong tree

3. **You barked up the wrong tree** by getting mad at her. She didn't do anything wrong.

   = ...

No sweat!

4. A: Thanks so much for looking after my children last Sunday.
   B: **No sweat**! I didn't have any plans, anyway. And I had a great time with them!

   = ...

* 또는 간단히 Use time wisely.

Be on vacation

5. A: Can I speak to Mr. Kim, please?

   B: I'm afraid **he's on vacation** now. He'll be back next Monday.

   = ...

C. Phrasal Verbs
: Take (...) up (...) / Check in / Check out

Try to guess the meaning of each phrasal verb before you watch the lecture.

> (Friends Talking)
> A: I didn't know you can play the guitar.
> B: I'm not good at it; **I just took it up** a month ago.

1. "Take (something) up (something)" means: ....

> (Wife to Husband in a Car)
> A: Let me get out here. **I'll check in** at the front desk while you park the car.
> B: Sounds good.

2. "Check in" means: ....

> (Wife to Husband at Front Desk)
> A: Honey, **I'll check out**. Why don't you take the kids to the car?
> B: Okay!

3. "Check out" means: ....

D. This is Confusing!

철수: 교수님, 벌써 마지막 수업이네요. 마지막 질문 드립니다. 얼마 전에 영화를 봤는데 별로 재미가 없었어요. 그래서 '지루했다'라고 표현하고 싶은데, 사전을 찾아봤더니 **bored**도 있고 **boring**도 있더라고요. 다른 의미로 사용되나요?

교수님: 좋은 질문입니다. 그럼 잘 들어보세요!

(Friends Chatting at Coffee Shop)

A: So how was the movie? I'll see it if you think it was good.

B: Actually, I don't recommend it. **It** was **bored**. (X)

→ Actually, I don't recommend it. **It** was **boring**. (O)

A: Everybody's talking about the new disaster movie. Did you see it?

B: Yeah, but **I** was pretty **disappointing**. (X) **The CGI** was quite **disappointed**. (X)

→ Yeah, but **I** was pretty **disappointed**. (O) **The CGI** was quite **disappointing**. (O)

LESSON 14

E. Variety / Register / Nuance: See (a movie) vs. Watch (TV)

See vs. Watch

A: Did you **see** James today? (see: one's physical ability)

B: No. Why?

A: Did you **watch** James today? (watch: observe movement or action)

B: No. Was I supposed to?

See/Watch a movie vs. Watch TV

A: What do you do in your free time / in your leisure time?

B: **I go to a theater and watch a movie**.

Compare **Let's go and see a movie**. (O) / I **watch a DVD**. (O)

A: How do you spend your evenings after work?

B: I usually eat dinner and **watch TV**. (O)

Compare I **see TV**. (X)

F. Word Parts : Suffixes (-al / -ist)

Base Word + -al / -ist = Noun Marker / Someone That Does Something

Survive (V) + -al	=	Survival (N)
Guitar (N) + -ist	=	Guitarist (N)

- I'll be living in the States for about six months. I'll learn some survival English.
- I recently started taking guitar lessons. I want to be a good guitarist some day.

Guess the meaning of each underlined word. Follow the three steps.

1. The criminal is still in denial. He keeps saying he didn't steal the diamonds.

   Step 1 : Denial = ...

   Step 2 : Denial = ... + ...

   Step 3 : Base Word Meaning = ...

2. She's a world-class violinist! Once you hear her play the violin, you'll become a fan of hers instantly!

   Step 1 : Violinist = ... + ...

   Step 2 : Base Word Meaning = ...

   Step 3 : New Word Meaning = ...

Jennifer: *Okay, guys! Are you ready to do our final role-play practice? If you're ready, here we go!*

1. **상황: 기말고사를 모두 마친 후에 친구와 함께 영화를 보러 가기로 함**

Friend: About what time should we arrive at the theater tomorrow?
(내일 몇 시쯤 극장에 도착하면 될까?)

You: ....
(제시간에 들어가려면 적어도 30분 일찍?)

Friend: Since we bought the tickets online, that'll be enough time.
(인터넷상으로 예매는 했으니까 시간은 충분하겠네.)

You: ....
(그럼 내일 5시쯤에 너희 집에 데리러 갈까?)

2. **상황: 레스토랑에 전화를 걸어 저녁 식사 테이블을 예약하려고 함**

You: ....
(오늘 저녁 6시에 예약을 하고 싶은데요, 사람은 3명입니다.)

Receptionist: I'm sorry but we're fully booked.
(죄송하지만 이미 다 찼네요.)

You: ....
(그럼 5시는 자리가 있나요?)

Receptionist: Let me see... Yes, we do. Shall we go ahead for 5?
(잠시만요…… 네, 자리가 있네요. 그럼 5시로 예약을 잡아드릴까요?)

3. **상황: 친한 동갑내기 직장 동료와 대화 중**

You: ....
(너 제이슨이랑 말다툼했다며?)

Colleague: Yeah. (응.)

You: ....
(근데 네가 오해하고 있는 거야.)

Colleague: What do you mean? (무슨 말이야?)

Jennifer: *On this last page, you'll do a final review of today's lesson. I'll read aloud five Korean sentences. Please express them in English, OK? Write sentences and check the example sentences.*

1. **저는 삼성 라이온즈 팬이에요.**

   ....

2. **우리나라가 일본에 3대 0으로 졌어요!**

   ....

3. **저는 요즘 재난영화에 관심이 가는 것 같더라고요(interest).**

   I think .... these days.

4. **여기서 드시고 가실 건가요, 아니면 포장인가요?**

   ....

5. **(이메일 자동 답변 메시지) 저는 지금 휴가 중이랍니다. 돌아오는 대로 답변 드리겠습니다.**

   ....

LESSON 1

THE VERB, HAVE

...

READ AND UNDERSTAND

저는 보통 매일 **아침에 식사를 해요**. 건강에는 아침을 먹는 게 정말 중요하잖아요. 그런데 가끔은 **아침을 많이 먹을 때가 있고**, 또 빨리 먹어요. 좋은 습관은 아니죠. 한번은 배탈이 났던 적도 있어요. 그리고 점식은 거르지 않아요. (점심에는) 주로 동료들과 밖에서 먹어요. 그리고 짧은 휴식을 취하죠. 인터넷으로 뉴스 기사를 읽어요. 이 시간에는 꿀을 넣은 **홍차를 즐겨 마셔요**. 저녁은 집에서 요리해서 먹는데 **가볍게 먹으려고 해요**. 밤에 **많이 먹으면** 건강에 안 좋으니까요.

...

QUESTIONS

1. 저는 보통 아침 식사를 하는 편인가요?
2. 사무실에서 저는 오랜 시간 휴식을 취하나요, 아니면 짧은 휴식을 취하나요?
3. 저는 어떤 차를 즐겨 마시나요?

LESSON 2

THE VERB, TAKE

...

READ AND UNDERSTAND

오늘 아침 7시에 일어났어요. 평상시처럼 한 시간 가량 **산책을 했죠**. 그리고 **샤워를 했어요**. 그런 후에는 아침을 푸짐하게 먹었고요. 10시쯤에 집을 나서서 **택시를 탔어요**. 보통은 출근할 때 **지하철을 타는데** 오늘은 너무 추웠거든요. 한양사이버대학교의 제 사무실에 도착해서는 커피를 한 잔 마셨어요. 그러고는 박 교수님께서 지시하신 일을 했어요. 아마도 아침을 많이 먹어서인지 점심 때가 되어도 배고프지가 않더라고요. 그래서 오후 6시까지 계속 일하다가 퇴근했어요. 긴 하루였지만 전혀 피곤하지는 않았어요. 제 생각에는 제가 가르치는 일을 좋아하나 봐요!

...

QUESTIONS

1. 저는 오늘 아침에 얼마나 오래 걸었나요?
2. 오늘 저는 왜 택시를 탔어요?
3. 저는 오늘 점심을 먹었나요?

LESSON 3

THE VERB, GO & COME

...

LISTEN AND UNDERSTAND

Mike: 지난 일요일에 굉장히 재미있었다며!

Jennifer: 응! **인사동에 갔거든**. 거기 가게들이 엄청 많더라!

Mike: **한 군데라도 들어가봤어**?

Jennifer: 당연하지. 재미있는 것도 샀는데.

Mike: 한번 보고 싶은데 **오늘 중에 너희 집에 가도 돼**?

Jennifer: 물론. 오늘은 **언제든지 가능해(언제든지 와도 돼)**.

Mike: 잘됐네! **가기 전에(=출발하기 전에) 전화할게**.

...

TRUE/FALSE STATEMENTS

1. 저는 오늘 인사동에 갔답니다.
2. Mike는 오늘 저희 집에 올 거예요.
3. 인사동의 어떤 가게에도 들어가지 않았어요.

LESSON 4

THE VERB, MAKE

...

READ AND UNDERSTAND

오늘 저는 우리 아름다운 어머니께서 젊으셨을 때에 대해 이야기할 거예요. 어머니께서는 매우 바쁘셨어요. (지금도 바쁘세요!) 사업을 하셨는데 피자 가게를 하셨어요. (바쁜데도 불구하고) 우리(자매)를 위해서 학교 가는 날에는 **세 끼를 항상 만들어주셨어요**. 동생*과 저는 학교에 점심 도시락을 항상 가져갔어요. 우리 어머니는 손재주가 뛰어났어요. **동생과 저의 인형들 옷과 원피스를 직접 만들어주셨거든요**. 어머니는 또한 매우 현명한 분이셨어요. **판단을 내려야 할 때는** 충분한 시간을 가지셨어요. 그래서 **실수를 많이 하지 않으셨어요**.

* sister는 언니, 여동생, 누나를 의미할 수 있지만 여기에서는 Jennifer의 여동생으로 해석한다.

...

TRUE/FALSE STATEMENTS

1. 우리 어머니는 피자 가게를 하셨답니다.
2. 우리 어머니는 학교 가는 날에는 매일 세 끼 식사를 요리해주셨어요.
3. 어머니는 실수를 많이 하셨답니다.

LESSON 5

THE VERB, DO

...

READ AND UNDERSTAND

여러분들도 아시겠지만 저는 매일 아침에 산책을 해요. **산책은 건강을 위해서 하는 건데요, 다른 운동들도 한답니다**. 오늘은 제가 어떤 운동들을 하고 있는지 얘기할게요. 저는 **토요일마다 요가를 한 시간 동안 해요**. 그런 후에는 한강을 따라서 자전거를 타죠. 몸이 무척 쌩쌩하고 가벼워지는 게 느껴져요! 그리고 **집안일을 할 때도 운동을 해요**. 예를 들어, **설거지를 할 때는** 발끝으로 서서 해요. 처음에는 어려웠지만 서서히 수월해졌어요. 마지막으로 저는 **암벽 타는 운동도 한답니다**. **이 운동은 자주 하지는 않지만** 스트레스 받을 때 **(암벽 등반을) 한답니다**. **이 운동을 하는 중에는** 걱정거리들을 잊어버리게 되거든요.

...

QUESTIONS

1. 저는 얼마나 자주 요가를 하나요?
2. 한강을 따라 저는 무엇을 하나요?
3. 저는 왜 암벽등반 운동을 할까요?

LESSON 6

THE VERB, GIVE

...

LISTEN AND UNDERSTAND

Jennifer: 이번 토요일에 강남에 가서 몇몇 학생들과 어울릴 계획이야.

Mike: 아, 강남 스타일로 어울린다고! (웃음)

Jennifer: 응, 강남 스타일. (웃음)

Mike: 사실은 나도 강남에서 5시에 친구 만나야 되는데.

Jennifer: 정말? 나도 5시에 학생들과 만나기로 했는데.

Mike: 잘됐다. **태워줄게**.

Jennifer: 고마워! 너 집 나서기 전에 **나한테 전화해줄 수 있어**?

...

TRUE/FALSE STATEMENTS

1. Mike와 저는 '강남 스타일'이라는 노래에 대해 알고 있답니다.
2. Mike가 운전을 해서 저를 태워줄 겁니다.
3. 저는 (집을) 나서기 전에 Mike에게 전화를 할 겁니다.

LESSON 7

THE VERB, GET

...

LISTEN AND UNDERSTAND

Jennifer: 다음 주는 우리 동생 생일이야. **뭘 좀 사주고 싶은데** 좋은 생각 있어?

Mike: 뭘 좋아하는데?

Jennifer: 우리 동생은 핸드백을 좋아해.

Mike: **그럼 멋진 핸드백을 하나 사주면 어때**?

Jennifer: 음, 그런데 한국은 여성 핸드백이 엄청 비싸.

Mike: 그래? 그럼 뭐 시간은 충분하니까 좀 더 생각해보면 되지.

QUESTIONS

1. 우리 동생은 생일이 언제인가요?
2. 동생은 어떤 것을 좋아하나요?
3. 저는 동생에게 핸드백을 사 줄 건가요?

LESSON 9

HEALTH & FEELINGS

...

READ AND UNDERSTAND

오늘 제가 마음이 상당히 불안해요. 왜 그런지 아세요? 중간고사가 오늘 시작되거든요. 제가 대학원생이라고 여러분들께 얘기해드렸던가요? 저는 영어교육을 전공하고 있답니다. 사실은 이번이 첫 학기라서 오늘 첫 시험을 치게 됐는데, **굉장히 초조하고 걱정이 되네요**. 아쉽게도 어젯밤에 푹 자지를 못했어요. **그래서 굉장히 피곤하기도 해요**. 그래도 **오늘 시험을 잘 쳐서 저 자신을 자랑스러워할 수 있으면 좋겠어요**. 사실 학업과 일을 병행한다는 건 쉬운 일이 아니잖아요. 하지만 이 두 가지 영역에서 최선을 다한다면 좋은 결과가 있을 거라고 생각한답니다.

...

TRUE/FALSE STATEMENTS

1. 저는 이번 학기에 졸업할 예정입니다.
2. 오늘은 굉장히 피곤해요. 왜냐하면 어젯밤에 푹 자지를 못했거든요.
3. 오늘 시험을 잘 봐서 저 자신이 자랑스럽게 느껴지면 좋겠어요.

LESSON 10

APPEARANCE & CHARACTER

...

LISTEN AND UNDERSTAND

Mike: 얘가 동생이야?

Jennifer: 응, 맞아. **예쁘지**?

Mike: 응. 그리고 **굉장히 친절한 인상이네**.

Jennifer: 친구들도 굉장히 많고 처음 보는 사람들과도 잘 어울려.

Mike: 그렇구나. **키도 꽤 큰 것 같은데**. **키가 어떻게 돼**?

Jennifer: 정확히는 모르겠지만 아마도 170 정도?

Mike: 우와! 그럼 **너보다 크네**.

...

TRUE/FALSE STATEMENTS

1. Mike는 과거에 제 동생을 만난 적이 있답니다.
2. 동생은 다른 사람들에게 말을 거는 것을(이야기하는 것을) 좋아합니다.
3. 저는 동생보다 키가 작습니다.

LESSON 11

WORK & OFFICE PROBLEMS

...

READ AND UNDERSTAND

여러분도 아시듯이 저는 대학원생이에요. 그리고 한양사이버대학교에서 **상근직으로 일하고 있어요**. 어떻게 그게 가능하냐고요? 온라인 대학원에 다니고 있거든요. 그래서 **학업과 일을 병행할 수가 있답니다**. 그런데 여러분들도 아시겠지만 이게 쉬운 일이 아니에요. **상근직이라서 9시에서 6시까지 근무를 해요**. 그래도 **저는 직장이 있다는 게 행복하답니다**. 왜냐하면 제 등록금은 제가 낼 수가 있고, (그리고) **요즘에는 취직을 하는 것이 굉장히 어렵잖아요**. 그리고 **저는 제 일을 좋아해요**! 전에도 말씀드렸듯이 저는 가르치는 일이 좋거든요. 그래서 불평할 수가 없어요. **그리고 내년에는 월급이 인상될 수도 있어요**! 그럼 **더 많은 돈을 벌 수 있을 거예요**. 만약에 그렇게 된다면 휴가는 미국으로 돌아가서 지낼 거랍니다!

...

TRUE/FALSE STATEMENTS

1. 저는 풀 타임 학생이고, 일은 비상근으로 하고 있습니다.
2. 저는 오프라인 대학원에서 공부하고 있어요.
3. 내년에는 돈을 더 벌 수 있을지도 모른답니다.

LESSON 12

TIME & PLACE

...

LISTEN AND UNDERSTAND

Jennifer: 잠깐만. **오늘 며칠이지**?

Mike: 몰라? **23일이잖아**.

Jennifer: 아빠 생신을 깜박할 번했네! **내일 모레거든**.

Mike: 그렇구나. 그런데 넌 요즘 괜찮아?

Jennifer: 무슨 말인지 알아. 내가…… 이런! **화장실에 스마트폰을 놓고 왔어**!

Mike: 오, Jennifer...

Jennifer: 잠깐만! 지갑이 어디 있지? **지하철에 놓고 내렸나**?

...

QUESTIONS

1. Mike는 오늘이 며칠인지 아나요?
2. 제 아버지의 생신은 언제인가요?
3. 제 스마트폰은 어디에 있나요?

LESSON 13

WEATHER & NATURAL DISASTERS

...

READ AND UNDERSTAND

오늘은 날씨에 대해서 이야기할 거예요. 여러분들은 어떤 날씨를 좋아하세요? **누구나 가장 좋아하는 유형의 날씨가 있어요**. 대부분의 사람들이 그렇듯이 **저는 밝고 화창한 날씨를 좋아해요. 하늘이 맑고 푸르면** 상쾌하고 산뜻한 느낌이 나요. 하지만 저는 **비 오는 날도 좋아한답니다**. 그런데 오해하지는 마세요! **빗속에 있는 걸** 좋아하는 건 아니고 **빗소리를 좋아해요**. 그러니까 **빗방울이 땅에 닿을 때 나는 소리가 좋아요**. **특히나 비가 세차게 올 때 말이죠**. 왠지 이런 소리를 들을 때면 스트레스가 확 풀리는 것 같거든요. 여러분은 어떠세요?

...

TRUE/FALSE STATEMENTS

1. 저는 비 오는 날씨를 좋아한답니다. 빗속에 있는 걸 좋아하거든요.
2. 저는 햇살이 가득한 날도 좋아해요. 왜냐하면 하늘이 맑고 파랗거든요.
3. 세차게 떨어지는 빗소리는 제 스트레스를 없애줘요.

LESSON 14

LEISURE & VACATIONS

...

LISTEN & UNDERSTAND

Jennifer: 우와, **골프채 좀 봐. 너 골프 치는 줄 몰랐어**!

Mike: 너도 알다시피 **미국은 골프 치는 게 그렇게 비싸지 않잖아**. 그래서 좀 배워뒀지.

Jennifer: 재미있겠다! 그러고 보니 이번 주말에 나 **야구 경기 보러 갈 건데**.

Mike: 그래? **어느 팀 응원할 건데**?

Jennifer: 나 삼성 라이온즈 **광팬**이야.

Mike: 지난 토요일에 **기아 타이거즈를 11대 10으로 이겼잖아**. 그렇지?

Jennifer: 응! 진짜 멋졌어!

...

TRUE/FALSE STATEMENTS

1. Mike는 한국에서 골프 치는 법을 배웠답니다.
2. 이번 주말에 저는 농구 경기를 보러 갈 겁니다.
3. 저는 기아 타이거즈를 응원합니다.

LESSON 1

THE VERB, HAVE

...

QUESTION OF THE DAY

Do you have breakfast every morning?

...

READ AND UNDERSTAND

1. Yes.
2. For a short time
3. Black tea

...

MAIN STORY

B. Idioms/Proverbs

1. be out of touch with the outside world, that is, be unrealistic or naive
2. be (romantically) interested in somebody (only)
3. be good at finding or recognizing something
4. tell a secret easily
5. like sweet flavor too much

C. Phrasal Verbs

1. 옷을 입고 있다.
2. 화장을 했거나 향수를 뿌리고 있다.

F. Word Parts

1. Step 1: dis+close
   Step 2: (문 등을) 닫다
   Step 3: 밝히다, 폭로하다
2. Step 1: 고용되지 않은, 직업이 없는
   Step 2: un+employed
   Step 3: 고용된/취업이 된 (Employ: 고용하다)

...

VOCABULARY USE IN DIALOG

1. Hi. / I have a cold. / Yeah.
2. I have a sweet tooth. / OK. I'll try to follow that.
3. Yeah. What is it? / she must have strong perfume on.

FINAL REVIEW

1. At my work, we have a meeting every Wednesday.
2. Have a beer.
3. I have a headache and a fever, too.
4. You have your head in the clouds again! (OR) Your head's in the clouds again!
5. She has a big mouth.

LESSON 2

THE VERB, TAKE

...

QUESTION OF THE DAY

Did you take (some) medicine?

...

READ AND UNDERSTAND

1. About an hour
2. Because it was very cold
3. No.

...

MAIN STORY

B. Idioms/Proverbs

1. Both people are responsible, not just one person.
2. Something else is more important.
3. do not hate something but do not particularly like it, either
4. do not value somebody/something because this person/thing is always there
5. unpleasant at first, but becomes better with time

C. Phrasal Verbs

1. 옷을 벗다/벗기다.
2. 신발을 벗다/벗기다.
3. 시간을 내서 1일 휴가를 얻다.

F. Word Parts

1. Step 1: non+native

   Step 2: 원어민의

   Step 3: 비원어민의

2. Step 1: 잘못 해석(이해)하다.

   Step 2: mis+interpret

   Step 3: 해석(이해)하다.

…

VOCABULARY USE IN DIALOG

1. I take the subway. / It takes (me) about 30 minutes. (OR) ...half an hour.
2. Well, these days, my family is taking a back seat. / I have to take my midterm exams this weekend.
3. Why don't you take this semester off?

…

FINAL REVIEW

1. I'm taking four classes this semester.
2. I'm taking cold medicine these days.
3. Let's take a break. Do you want a cup of coffee?
4. Take a thicker/warmer jacket with you.
5. Could you please take a picture of us?

LESSON 3

THE VERBS, GO & COME

…

QUESTION OF THE DAY

Can I come to your office?

(OR) Can I go to your office?

…

LISTEN AND UNDERSTAND

1. F
2. T
3. F

…

MAIN STORY

B. Idioms/Proverbs

1-1. be very successful

1-2. have known each other for many years

2. make great progress
3. suddenly or immediately think of something
4. can't think of anything
5. If a situation becomes very serious or difficult

C. Phrasal Verbs

1. (무슨 일이) 일어나다/벌어지다.
2. (무슨 일이) 계속해서 일어나다/벌어지다.
3. 서둘러! (상대방을 독려하고 있음)
4. 에이, 멀쩡한데. (상대방이 과장하고 있음을 함축)

F. Word Parts

1. Step 1: im+polite

   Step 2: 정중한, 예의 바른

   Step 3: 무례한

2. Step 1: 글을 읽거나 쓸 줄 모르는

   Step 2: il+literate

   Step 3: 글을 읽거나 쓸 줄 아는

…

VOCABULARY USE IN DIALOG

1. Does Bus No. 100 go downtown? / Thank you very much!
2. When should I come to your office? (OR) When should I go to your office?
3. my mind just went blank!

…

FINAL REVIEW

1. I'm going to go hiking on Sunday.
2. This product comes in two designs.
3. If (the) worst comes to (the) worst, I'll just sell my piano.
4. What's going on?
5. it went on snowing all day.

LESSON 4

THE VERB, MAKE

...

QUESTION OF THE DAY

Who makes dinner at your home?

...

READ AND UNDERSTAND

1. T
2. T
3. F

...

MAIN STORY

B. Idioms/Proverbs

1. make you happy
2. produce a certain look on your face to show that you do not like someone or something
3. make a decision
4. become very good at something if you keep doing it
5. If you want to be treated well, you should treat other people well, too.

C. Phrasal Verbs

1. -을 대신해서 채우다/보상하다/만회하다.
2. (-와) 화해하다.

F. Word Parts

1. Step 1: 격식을 차리지 않은, 언어가 일상적인
   Step 2: in+formal
   Step 3: 격식을 차린, 공식적인
2. Step 1: 무책임한
   Step 2: ir+responsible
   Step 3: 책임감 있는

...

VOCABULARY USE IN DIALOG

1. I'll make dinner and tea.
2. Stop making that face! / Apologize to her. Now!
3. Thanks for working the night shift for me! / How can I make it up to you?

...

FINAL REVIEW

1. Don't make noise, okay?
2. My children always make me smile.
3. Both are good. I can't make up my mind.
4. we should make a careful decision.
5. make more money

LESSON 5

THE VERB, DO

...

QUESTION OF THE DAY

I'm a teacher.

...

READ AND UNDERSTAND

1. Once a week (OR) Every Saturday
2. I go biking. (OR) I ride a bike.
3. To forget about my worries

...

MAIN STORY

B. Idioms/Proverbs

1. do what I want to do without following other people's ideas
2. It is not easy to earn/get money.
3. People need more than physical things such as food, houses, and money.
4. Don't be so sure about the results of something. Wait until it actually happens.
5. Make sure you have some alternatives.

C. Phrasal Verbs

1. -을 다시 하다.
2. -을 없애다/버리다.

F. Word Parts

1. Step 1: re+paint
   Step 2: -을 칠하다

Step 3: -을 다시 칠하다

2. Step 1: 필요 이상의 자격을 갖춘, 과분한

   Step 2: over+qualified

   Step 3: 자격이 있는

...

VOCABULARY USE IN DIALOG

1. What do you do?
2. I do the dishes for every meal.
3. money doesn't grow on trees.

...

FINAL REVIEW

1. Did you do a good job (OR) Did you do well
2. How's your business doing/going/coming along?
3. I hate doing the dishes!
4. Does this brand do sportswear only?
5. Man does not live by bread alone.

LESSON 6

THE VERB, GIVE

...

QUESTION OF THE DAY

Give me a big smile. (more common)

(OR) Smile broadly. (less common)

...

LISTEN AND UNDERSTAND

1. T
2. T
3. F

...

MAIN STORY

B. Idioms/Proverbs

1. willing to give something to others and to receive something from others
2. help someone
3. bother someone, make someone suffer
4. give a yes sign so someone can start something
5. decide to believe someone although s/he still has doubt

C. Phrasal Verbs

1. (성공하지 못할 것이라고 생각하여) 포기하다.
2. (건강에 좋지 않은 습관, 술 등)을 멈추다, 그만 마시다.

F. Word Parts

1. Step 1: ex+wife

   Step 2: 아내

   Step 3: 전처

2. Step 1: pre

   Step 3: 예측하다, 예견하다.

...

VOCABULARY USE IN DIALOG

1. I'll give you a ride.
2. I'll give you a call back later!
3. I'll give you the benefit of the doubt.

...

FINAL REVIEW

1. Can you give this book to James?

   (OR) Can you give James this book?

2. My dad gave me a big hug.
3. Can I give you a hand with anything?
4. Professor Kim is going to give an offline lecture
5. giving your brother a hard time!

LESSON 7

THE VERB, GET

...

QUESTION OF THE DAY

I'm getting married tomorrow.

...

LISTEN AND UNDERSTAND

1. Next week
2. Handbags
3. No.

...

MAIN STORY

B. Idioms/Proverbs

1. One does not express things directly, but you understand him/her.
2. understand a situation (by yourself or by hearing from someone)
3. don't want to continue doing something because you get afraid or nervous
4. find the truth about a situation
5. contact someone by calling or writing (including e-mail)

C. Phrasal Verbs

1. (잠자리에서) 일어나다/깨우다.
2. (매일 같은) 버스/지하철/기차를 타다.
3. (타고 있던) 버스/지하철/기차에서 내리다.

F. Word Parts

1. Step 1: anti+social
   Step 2: 사회의, 사교적인
   Step 3: 반사회적인
2. Step 1: sub+marine
   Step 2: 바다의
   Step 3: 바닷속의, 잠수함

...

VOCABULARY USE IN DIALOG

1. Look at the camera over there! / I'm getting hungry.
2. get our tickets
3. She wasn't interested in me. / So I got the message.

...

FINAL REVIEW

1. I got a letter from my boyfriend.
2. Could I get you anything?
3. I usually get home at midnight.
4. I need to get in touch with John.
5. Can you go and get your dad up?

LESSON 9

HEATH & FEELINGS

...

QUESTION OF THE DAY

I'm very worried about the exam results.
(OR) I'm very worried about my exam results.

...

READ AND UNDERSTAND

1. F
2. T
3. T

...

MAIN STORY

B. Idioms/Proverbs

1. have both positive and negative feelings
2. be happy/be angry or depressed
3. feel that you want to do something
4. be bored with or annoyed by something/someone
5. Don't feel sad or depressed. More chances will come.

C. Phrasal Verbs

1. 기운을 내다 / ~의 기분을 띄워주다.
2. 진정하다 / ~를 안정시키다

F. Word Parts

1. Step 1: 안락한, 편안한
   Step 2: comfort+able
   Step 3: 안락, 편안
2. Step 1: 보통, 정상적으로
   Step 2: normal+ly
   Step 3: 보통의, 정상적인

...

VOCABULARY USE IN DIALOG

1. I have heartburn and a little indigestion. / About a week ago
2. I like romantic comedies. / What kind of movie do you like?
3. I'm not in the mood for talking / to talk.

...

FINAL REVIEW

1. Come inside and get warm!
2. I still have a hangover.
3. you still have a temperature.
4. I'm so stressed (out) these days.
5. I cut/nicked my finger.

LESSON 10

APPEARANCE & CHARACTER

...

QUESTION OF THE DAY

He is a very nice / really good person.

(OR) She is a very nice / really good person.

...

LISTEN AND UNDERSTAND

1. F
2. T
3. T

...

MAIN STORY

B. Idioms/Proverbs

1. like/unlike one's usual character
2. manage/fail to control one's anger
3. an ordinary person
4. People have different thoughts about what is beautiful.
5. Don't judge people or things based on how they look outside.

C. Phrasal Verbs

1. 옷을 좀 더 멋지게/격식 있게 차려 입다.
2. 자랑하다.

F. Word Parts

1. Step 1: forget+ful

   Step 2: 잊다

   Step 3: 잘 잊어먹는, 건망증이 있는
2. Step 1: -ous → Adjective

   Step 3: 음식이 맛있는

...

VOCABULARY USE IN DIALOG

1. Can I give you some advice? / be so honest / frank with other people

   (OR) Don't be too open / too trusting.
2. You were so mean to me.
3. Well, you can't always judge a book by its cover. / They're so stubborn!

...

FINAL REVIEW

1. She's so humble. (OR) He's so humble.
2. She's very sociable. (OR) He's very sociable.
3. Don't be childish, OK?
4. A lazy person can never succeed in life.
5. You're really dressed up today!

LESSON 11

WORK & OFFICE PROBLEMS

...

QUESTION OF THE DAY

Would you consider giving me a raise?

...

READ AND UNDERSTAND

1. F
2. F
3. T

...

MAIN STORY

B. Idioms/Proverbs

1. (praise) do something well
2. You work too much and do not take time to relax.
3. It is OK with me.
4. If several people help one person with a large task, they can finish it easily and quickly.
5. Time resolves everything.

C. Phrasal Verbs

1. (건강/몸매 관리를 위해) 운동하다.
2. 노력을 들여서 (어떤 일을) 하다.

F. Word Parts

1. Step 1: 소비자

   Step 2: consume+(e)r

   Step 3: 소비하다
2. Step 1: 선원, 뱃사람

   Step 2: sail+or

   Step 3: 항해하다

…

VOCABULARY USE IN DIALOG

1. So, you're a news anchor. / but … you want to quit your job?
2. I work for a small company. / I have two children.
3. This week, I'm doing the night shift. / That's alright, mom.

…

FINAL REVIEW

1. I work at Samsung.

   (OR) I work for Samsung.
2. This job involves a lot of talking.
3. This photocopier is not working again!
4. Don't worry. Time works wonders.
5. I work out every day.

LESSON 12

TIME & PLACE

…

QUESTION OF THE DAY

What time is it now?

(OR) Do you have the time?

…

LISTEN AND UNDERSTAND

1. Yes.
2. The 25th
3. In the restroom

…

MAIN STORY

B. Idioms/Proverbs

1. Time passes very quickly.
2. I haven't seen you in a long time.
3. speak with someone at an inconvenient time for him/her
4. Time is finished.
5. Time is as important as money, so don't waste it.

C. Phrasal Verbs

1. (사람들과) 시간을 보내다.
2. (사람들과) 만나서 시간을 함께 보내다.

F. Word Parts

1. Step 1: 생산적인, 결실 있는

   Step 2: produce+ive

   Step 3: 생산, 산출, 창조하다.
2. Step 1: 먼지투성이의

   Step 2: dust+y

   Step 3: 먼지

…

VOCABULARY USE IN DIALOG

1. Let's meet at the coffee shop on the first floor. / It's in Cyber Building 2.
2. What are you doing now? / It's 11: 59pm the day after tomorrow.
3. Time flies. / I didn't do well on the midterm exams

···

FINAL REVIEW

1. What date is today?
   (OR) What date is it today?
2. Today's October 20th.
   (OR) It's October 20th.
3. I was born in (the) winter.
4. the next bus will come in 10 minutes.
5. Where are you? Are you behind the curtains? (OR) Are you hiding behind the curtains?

LESSON 13

WEATHER & NATURAL DISASTERS

···

QUESTION OF THE DAY

A rain shower just started!

···

READ AND UNDERSTAND

1. F
2. T
3. T

···

MAIN STORY

B. Idioms/Proverbs

1. feel a little sick
2. someone who is a friend only when you are happy or successful
3. suspected of having done something wrong
4. It's raining very heavily.
5. Although one is having difficulties now, s/he will be successful in the end.

C. Phrasal Verbs

1. (운동이나 활동 전에) 몸을 가볍게 풀어주다.
2. (날씨가) 개다.

F. Word Parts

1. Step 1: employ+ment
   Stop 2: 고용하다.
   Step 3: 고용
2. Step 1: 굶주림
   Step 2: starve+tion
   Step 3: 굶주리다.

···

VOCABULARY USE IN DIALOG

1. Really? Is it going to be hot? / for me to start on a diet then!
2. I'm not sure, but we can check it on my smartphone! / No need to worry – no rain. / It says it's going to be just a little cloudy.
3. Nice weather we're having, huh? / Where are you from?

···

FINAL REVIEW

1. it's going to be overcast today
2. I hate muggy/sultry days. (OR) My least favorite weather is muggy/sticky weather.
3. It's raining cats and dogs!
4. There's light at the end of the tunnel, so let's be patient!
5. It's very important to warm up before we work out!

LESSON 14

LEISURE & VACATIONS

···

QUESTION OF THE DAY

What's your favorite movie genre?

···

LISTEN AND UNDERSTAND

1. F
2. F

3. F

...

MAIN STORY

B. Idioms/Proverbs

1. at a convenient time
2. The busiest men find the most time for leisure.
3. You blame someone for doing something, but you have the wrong person.
4. No problem! / It was easy! / You're welcome!
5. time off from work

C. Phrasal Verbs

1. (운동이나 취미를) 시작하다.
2. (호텔 등에서) 투숙 수속을 밟다, 체크인하다.
3. (호텔 등에서) 돈을 지불하고 퇴실 수속을 밟다, 체크아웃하다.

F. Word Parts

1. Step 1: 부정, 부인
   Step 2: deny+al
   Step 3: 부정하다, 인정하지 않다.
2. Step 1: violin+ist
   Step 2: 바이올린
   Step 3: 바이올린 연주자

...

VOCABULARY USE IN DIALOG

1. To be safe, at least 30 minutes in advance? / Then I'll pick you up at your place at about 5pm?
2. I'd like to make a reservation for three people at 6pm tonight. / Then, do you have a table available for 5pm?
3. I hear you had an argument with Jason. / But you barked up the wrong tree.

...

FINAL REVIEW

1. I'm a fan of the Samsung Lions.
2. We lost to Japan 0 to 3!
3. I'm interested in disaster movies.
   (OR) I'm into disaster movies.
4. For here or to go?
5. I'm on vacation now. I'll get back to you as soon as possible.

박수정

계명대학교 미국학(부전공: 영어영문학) 학사

미국 University of Nebraska at Lincoln 학부 교환학생 프로그램 이수

미국 University of Illinois at Urbana-Champaign 영어교육학 석사/박사

미국 University of Illinois at Urbana-Champaign 산하 ESL 프로그램 강사

미국 University of Illinois at Urbana-Champaign MATESL 대학원 강의교수

현 한양사이버대학교 영어학과 전임교수

—

[공저]

HYCU College English 1

NEW PATH 2 - Practical Guide to General English

BASIC VOCABULARY
IN EVERYDAY ENGLISH

펴낸날 2015년 12월 30일 초판 1쇄 ● 2021년 3월 30일 초판 3쇄

지은이 박수정 ● **펴낸이** 김우승

펴낸곳 한양대학교출판부 ● **출판등록** 제4-7호(1972.2.29)

주소 서울 성동구 왕십리로 222 ● **전화** 02.2220.1432-4 ● **팩스** 02.2220.1435

홈페이지 press.hanyang.ac.kr ● **이메일** presshy@hanyang.ac.kr

디자인 안광일 ● **인쇄** 미르P&P

값 11,000원

ISBN 978.89.7218.477.5 (03740)